ENDORSE

"Julie King is a passionate follower of Jesus who embraces a
see her sisters in Christ set free from fear, pain, and bondage of every kind so that they may rise up and passionately follow Jesus. God is using Julie mightily as she calls upon women to awaken and arise and embrace their respective destinies, allowing God to empower them as salt and light in order to transform this dark world through the light and love of Christ. This book reveals Julie's heart for her sisters in Christ, challenging them to see their worth and calling and spiritual authority through God's eyes and, ultimately, to fulfill that purpose by proclaiming the gospel to the nations. As you pray, read, and worship your way through this book, may you be supernaturally 'transformed into his image with ever-increasing glory, which comes from the Lord, who is the Spirit (2 Corinthians 3:18).'" **Kurt Nelson, President and CEO, East-West Ministries International**

"Julie is a breath of fresh air in a culture quickly becoming less authentic and more image-focused. She draws women into a deep and bold relationship with Jesus through her life, leadership, and expeditions into the ends of the earth. With this devotional offering, Julie bids you to join her in the journey of seeking the heart of God. Her words and revelation will leave you with the lingering fragrance of her overflowing heart of worship." **Jenny Erlingsson, founder of Milk & Honey Women and author of "Becoming His"**

"Julie's passion for the Scriptures is contagious. Your heart's affections for Jesus will be amplified with this incredible resource designed to immerse you in the Scriptures and bring you closer to the heart of God." **Kat Armstrong, preacher and co-founder of Polished Ministries and author of "No More Holding Back"**

"As these daily devotions are studied and applied, the Holy Spirit breathes life into the heart and spirit of the reader. I have not experienced God so intimately or powerfully through many other writings, other than the Bible. Prepare to be touched, challenged, commissioned, and elevated to a higher level of intimacy and mission with God through this 31-day journey. You will be forever changed." **Mary Ethel Eckard, co-founder of Dragonfly Ministries and author of "The Making of a Dragonfly, Following Christ Through the Winds of Change"**

"Julie has mastered helping people move into more intimacy with Jesus because she is the chief learner. We are all worshipers at our core, and her devotionals invite you into the moments with the Lord where the mountains of life get moved and hearts get shaped. Women need these moments to remind them that they daily carry in them the life of Jesus - the power of life change. He wants to live His life in and through each one of us, and He desperately wants to have these one-on-one conversations to tell us how." **J. Mitchell Little, Partner, Scheef & Stone, LLP**

"Julie's book 'Arise My Darling' accomplishes in print what this author does in person. Through the lens of Scripture and with the heart of Jesus, Julie has a unique ability to draw out prayer in each of us. Give yourself 31 days to be mentored, discipled, and released to move forward to unlocking prayer in you. Listen and linger as you hear God's voice speak to you personally. Then give way to what you have been given." **Mary Jo Pierce, Pastor at Gateway Church and author of "Adventures in Prayer: 40 Day Journey" and "Follow Me: An Unending Conversation with Jesus"**

"Julie takes us on a journey through her own time spent in the secret place. In these 31 days, the Lord brings us back to the basics to our reason for existence - to worship and be in communion with Him. He draws us more and more into His heart and shows us what it means to be intimately loved by a passionate God. Whether you find yourself feeling the closest you have ever felt to Him or the furthest away, get ready to feel a new fire ignited and passion for the One so deep, you can't contain it." **Lizzy King, RN, worship leader and singer/ songwriter**

"Julie writes with a beauty and intimacy that flows directly out of her relationship with Jesus and the desire He's given her for others to experience Him deeply. Not only is her writing real, authentic, and directly from her time with the Lord, it encourages you to go to Jesus yourself and see Him more clearly for who He really is - the one your soul longs for more than any other. I have loved getting a glimpse into the depth of Julie's relationship with Jesus. And I love the purity of devotion through each day. What a beautiful peek into deep intimacy with Jesus and what He desires for us all!" **Matt Smith, Pastor of the Online Experience, Bent Tree Bible Fellowship**

"You were designed to worship. 'Arise My Darling' will ignite your passion to encounter Jesus more fully and to be consumed by His everlasting love. Lingering with Him in this 31-day devotional that is lavishly bathed in scriptural truths and wisdom, you will experience the intimacy, wonder, and glory of worshiping Jesus afresh. Julie has generated a call to action to live for Christ, as her own life has so beautifully modeled, and to share our Savior's outrageous grace through unleashed engagement with others. Let's get moving, beloved sisters!" **Cindy Brinker Simmons, board member of East-West Ministries International and Dallas Theological Seminary and author of "Little Mo's Legacy: A Mother's Lessons, A Daughter's Story"**

"Fall into the glorious richness of who you are in Christ. Julie King once again calls women to abandon themselves to the overwhelming wonder of the Father's heart. This is a call to go deeper and higher in your journey with Father God, connecting with His love for you like never before!" **Autumn Ross, Co-Founder and Executive Vice President, A. Larry Ross Communications**

ARISE

my Darling

Encounters with Jesus
to Ignite Passion, Worship,
and Wonder

JULIE KING

A 31-DAY DEVOTIONAL JOURNEY

Arise My Darling
Encounters with Jesus to Ignite Passion, Worship, and Wonder
Julie King | East-West Publishing

To contact the author: jking@eastwest.org

For updated information on events, trips, resources, and ways to get involved, visit our website at www.eastwest.org/arise

ISBN (Print): 978-0-578-66327-2

East-West Publishing
Plano, TX

Jacket design by JOSEP Designs

DEDICATION

I dedicate this book to Michael King, who does everything in his power to see his girls soar. You have been the greatest example of what it means to lay your life down for another. Thanks for setting the bar high for our daughters. I honor you and love you deeply.

I also dedicate this book to our four warrior daughters who run breathlessly after Jesus. Lizzy, Emily, AnnMarie, and Grace, may your entire lives be an ignition point for the power and passion of God to flow in and through. He is your everything, and I am honored to run in lock step with you to our finish line - Christ Himself.

SPECIAL THANKS

I have spent recent years focused on the honor and privilege of being raised by two parents who said a radical *"YES"* to an outlandish call from God to serve Him. Their *"YES"* has changed nations and shifted generations. I am forever grateful for the impact of your *"YES"* on my life and the lives of my daughters. Forever I will honor you. I love you, Mom and Dad.

I want to especially thank the leadership of East-West Ministries International for believing in the call, identity, and authority by the Spirit to women in this hour. You believe women will change history, and you put something behind that belief. Thank you for investing vision, resources, leadership, and encouragement to see women come alive for the sake of the gospel.

To the 318 women who courageously said *"YES"* to an initial month-long fast, your faith spurred on my devotion and wonder of a God who fulfills His promises. What He speaks, He fulfills. You were evidence of that for me. Because you said *"YES,"* this book came to life.

FOREWORD

More than 8,000 miles away from home, I stood next to Julie King as she boldly shared the gospel message with an elderly couple in a remote area of the Himalayan Mountains. After 28 hours of flying, a 10-hour car ride, and seemingly countless miles of hiking, we had arrived at a village where we met a couple who had never before heard the name of Jesus. Julie shared the story of Jesus in English and her message was interpreted by one translator into one language and then by another translator to get the message into the local language this couple could understand. As I watched her share, I prayed. In that moment, I was overcome by joy at the blessing of partnering in the ministry of the gospel with this dear sister. I could see her heart aching for these two precious people to say *"YES"* to Jesus.

In God's great grace, this elderly couple professed faith in Jesus and prayed to receive Jesus as their Savior. The transformation that occurred in those moments was significant as they stepped from the kingdom of darkness into the kingdom of light. And standing right next to them, Julie beamed with joy at the eternal hope these two had just received.

What I have come to learn about Julie is that this was not just a mission trip experience. This aching, this desire for people to more fully know Jesus, is her longing every single day. And it is this longing for the Bride of Christ and unbelievers alike to draw nearer to Jesus that serves as the foundation of her life and of this book.

A Life Marked by the Gospel

As I have walked with Julie over the past couple of years, I have witnessed the life of a sister and friend who seeks to be radically obedient to God's leading because of the impact of the gospel in her life.

This lifestyle begins with her passionate pursuit of Jesus. Julie is fueled by her time alone with God and in His Word. She speaks with wisdom and authority as a result of her deep and abiding walk with Jesus. She acts as the Holy Spirit leads.

At the same time, Julie allows Jesus to pursue her. She goes before the Lord with an open spirit, seeking to be refined, sharpened, and shaped into the woman God is creating her to be for His Kingdom purposes.

Julie possesses incredible God-given faith. She trusts whole-heartedly in her Savior to work in her own life, in the lives of her brothers and sisters, and among the nations. Her belief in God's relentless pursuit of His people compels her to step into the unknown and trust the Holy Spirit's leading to fulfill His purposes.

Finally, Julie purposefully lives out the Great Commission. God's command in Matthew 28 to *"go and make disciples"* is not received by Julie as optional. She takes God at His word and intentionally disciples other women to also be disciples. In response to Acts 1:8, she seeks to be a witness from her Jerusalem all the way to the ends of the earth.

God's Heart for Revival

In church history, we see that all great revivals begin with a personal revival. As Charles Finney said, "Revival is a renewed conviction of sin and repentance, followed by an intense desire to live in obedience to God. It is giving up one's will to God in deep humility." In "Arise My Darling", Julie points us to God's heart for sustained personal revival, giving up our will to God and responding to the leading of the Spirit in radical obedience.

We know from God's Word that our Heavenly Father desires *"everyone to come to repentance (2 Peter 3:9)."* He desires a global revival by which all nations worship Him as King – and, oh, how deserving He is of such a revival. The most amazing part is that God's design allows for us - you and me - to be a part of this great work of revival. Romans 10:14-15 tells of our role: *"And how can they hear without someone preaching to them? And how can anyone preach unless they are sent? As it is written: 'How beautiful are the feet of those who bring good news!'"* We get to be messengers of the gospel to spark new revival among those who have yet to experience God's redeeming work in their lives. This devotional book equips us to more intentionally join God's mission to build His Church.

While God desires to use us for His work, the outcomes do not rest on our shoulders. The Holy Spirit is not only our Guide but also the One accomplishing the revival work in the hearts of those we seek to disciple and of the unbelievers. As Corrie ten Boom said, "Trying to do the Lord's work in your own strength is the most confusing, exhausting, and tedious of all work. But when you are filled with the Holy Spirit, then the ministry of Jesus just flows out of you." In this book, Julie lovingly guides us in learning how to listen to the voice of the Spirit that we might go about our lives with the ministry of Jesus flowing out of us.

As you read through these pages, my dear sisters, my prayer is that you would find complete freedom in God's deep love for you, so that you might be fully free to live in His purposes for your life. He desires all of you. May you approach these daily readings with open hands and open hearts, ready to receive all that God has in store for the days ahead for you. And as you lean into God's heart for you, be bold in sharing with others about His redemptive work with the same kind of passion and boldness that my dear sister, Julie, displayed on that Himalayan mountainside 8,000 miles away from home. Let us awake to the revival that God seeks to accomplish in and through each of our lives!

Kristen Shuler
Friend and Partner in the Gospel with Julie King
Executive Vice President of Development, East-West Ministries International

How to Use this Book

As I set out to write each devotional, I spent significant time in worship. Each worship song was perfectly matched with the devotional for that day. At the bottom of each day, you will see a song you can find on YouTube. Simply type in the exact title to find it. This will give you the context for what the Holy Spirit showed me to write and prepare for you for that day. The two things fit hand in hand.

In preparation of going through this book in conjunction with a time of fasting, here are just a few suggestions for you. (If you have health issues, please consult with a physician before committing to a 31-day fast.)

- **Regular fast** - Refrain from all food. Most people drink water or juice during a regular fast.
- **Partial fast** - Omit a specific meal from your diet or refrain from certain types of foods.
- **Liquid fast** - Eliminate solid food, but allow for water, juice, and broth.
- **Full or complete fast** - Consume no food and no drink.
- **Fast from worldly desires** - For example, give up coffee, soda, social media, entertainment, etc.

I recommend using the Reflection pages inserted in this book to write what the Holy Spirit shows you. Have your Bible in hand to read from additional translations you particularly love. I recommend creating ample space daily to get away and spend time with the Lord. Find a quiet space in your house that is free from distractions. This may mean you wake up earlier than normal.

You may need to **slow down** in order to set a new pace. Continue to linger with the Lord, minister to His heart, love Him, and He will show up in your hunger. On some of the days, I wrote what I heard from the Holy Spirit. On some of the devotionals, you will see where I've written that I've heard directly from the Lord on something. It is my heart for you to develop a confidence in knowing that He speaks to you. He is relational, and intimate, and communicative. We are trained to recognize His voice, and He promises that we do indeed hear it (John 10:27).

Use all six senses to encounter God. Below are ways that the Lord can speak to you by His Spirit. I have adapted this from Lana Vawser's book "The Prophetic Voice of God" [i]:

1. He will always speak through His Word. He will never contradict Himself.
2. He can appear before us like He did in Acts 9.
3. He can speak in an audible voice like He did in 1 Samuel.
4. He speaks in the still small voice, an internal voice into our hearts and minds. (I have found in learning to hear Him that I often dismiss His voice as my own because it's the most familiar voice to us without even recognizing it.)
5. The beauty of creation testifies to God Himself (Romans 1:19-20).
6. He speaks through visions and dreams (Numbers 12:6; Acts 22:17-18).
7. He can speak through impressions or through a knowing.

8. He also speaks through numbers, symbols, signs, newspaper headlines, movies, songs, circumstances, books, and others.

I want to encourage you to **write everything down**. Write down the vivid dreams you have at night. If they are full of color and you wake up remembering them with clarity, it's likely a God-dream. Write it down, date it, and try to give it a title.

The Lord has been speaking to me with numbers. I saw 3:33 on the clock every day for months. I finally asked the Lord what He was saying. He responded, "Jeremiah 33:3." **Take notice of the repetition of things, and don't dismiss them as coincidental. This is crucial.**

Last May, a bird built a nest on our tilted mailbox. It was the first time in six years, so I knew God was saying something. I scoured the Word, and He showed me exactly what He was saying. He spoke through creation and Scripture.

Be wide-eyed, ears open, looking, talking to the Lord, and writing things down as they come to mind. If you see a vivid picture in your mind or a series of pictures that look like a movie reel, that's a vision. Write it down and ask the Lord what He is saying. If it feels so weird and random, don't dismiss it. Take note. God will reveal what He is showing you. If your spouse or children begin to have dreams, write them down. Be all ears these 31 days.

I am so thankful you are joining me in this journey. Enjoy the time and space with the Lord. Enjoy Him. Enjoy His presence. He is about to pour out wonder upon wonder in this season. He has said to me over and over, "Jules, stay in your place of **joyous expectation**!" So, I pass that on to you.

Here we go …

CONTENTS

INTRODUCTION

It is time for the Bride to arise; both men and women, young and old. A dying world is awaiting an encounter with the Living God through your life and mine. As I sat with the Lord one morning, this Scripture came to life: *"The bride belongs to the bridegroom. The friend who attends the bridegroom waits and listens for him and is full of joy when he hears the bridegroom's voice" (John 3:29).*

Everything in me wanted that Scripture to bear witness in my life - the one who is wide awake, watching and listening for Him. But I needed not do this alone. I longed that, together, we would press in for an awakening of passion, worship, and revelation. As we enter a new decade, I believe there is an invitation to listen to what is on His heart for the Bride. So I called a fast, under the prompting of the Holy Spirit. It was a Joshua 3:5 moment in my spirit: *"Consecrate yourselves, for tomorrow the Lord will do amazing things among you."*

I had the number 200 in my heart. I believe the Lord wanted many more to come. In the end, I counted 318 hungry women who took the month of January 2020 to worship and sit with Him for breakthrough, revelation, healing, victory, freedom, wisdom, and insight. Every day I submitted to them something from my own time with Jesus. It was authentic, vulnerable, intimate, and timely. I would hear the Holy Spirit speak through Scripture to my spirit, and I would write. Enclosed between these two covers are 31 significant times with my

Father, my Jesus, and my beloved Holy Spirit. They are encounters of worship, wonder, and passion.

The mission statement of my life is to be a conduit of the passion and pursuit of Jesus for the sake of revival to both His Bride and to those who do not know Him. It's my immense joy in this season to both disciple women and to take them to the nations, which are His inheritance. We get to share in a bold proclamation and demonstration of the gospel to the ends of the earth. We speak and declare of the wonderous love of Christ to those who, for many, have never heard His name. I am watching women awake to a new level of love for Jesus and His heart for the world. I am watching women fall in love with their Bridegroom and stretching out to partner with all He is doing in the world. As Kris Vallotton says, "This is the most exciting time to be alive!" I agree. There is a wooing from the throne room of heaven to see what He sees and to partner with Him to bring heaven to earth.

My prayer for these next 31 days is that you become enraptured by a new level of intimacy and wonder with your Bridegroom. He is longing to take you to places in His heart you have yet to traverse. He is longing to show you the depth of freedom and victory He paid for you on the cross. He is waiting to reveal the hidden treasures He has in store for you in this next decade that will spur revival in and through your very life. Sit with Him and feast because there is much in store for His extraordinary Bride.

"Arise, my dearest. Hurry, my darling. Come away with me! I have come as you have asked to draw you to my heart and lead you out. For now is the time, my beautiful one."
-Song of Songs 2:10, TPT

Julie King

DAY

1

ARE YOU READY? HERE WE GO!

Jesus is calling us to position ourselves at the threshold of a new era with great expectation. He is inviting us to move forward with faith, vision, hope, and great joy.

"I slept but my heart was awake. Listen! My beloved is knocking: 'Open to me, my sister, my darling, my dove, my flawless one. My head is drenched with dew, my hair with the dampness of the night.'"
-Song of Solomon 5:2

That's the divine romance - the waiting, wooing, and calling of Jesus to His daughters, His Bride, in this hour. And we respond. We open the door of expectation and find Him standing there. He longs to embrace and speak and reveal and enlarge and expand and heal and move. There are no limitations to an encounter with the resurrected Jesus. He will come as He has promised.

As you begin these 31 days of devotions, prayer, and fasting, may He prepare your heart for what is coming in the days ahead. He has much to say and much to show.

Pray this prayer of consecration:

> Lord, I position my heart today to be in step with You. Confirm Your Word as we walk and talk together these next 31 days. I invite You to breakthrough in encounter with me so I may know and see and experience You in ways I have never done or heard or seen. I pray that doubt, insecurity, timidity, fear, and disappointment would have no root in my pursuit of You or my reception of You. I pray for a depth of faith and intimacy to be born in my life. Magnify Your invitation to intimacy in my heart. Call me into deep places in You, Lord, and give me the courage to traverse those places with You. I place my own heart before You - every part to be seen by You. I want nothing else to consume my heart, my desires, my longings, my cravings, and my passions but You, Jesus. I want to walk and dance in friendship with You, Jesus. I invite You to take me to new heights and depths of revelation and intimacy. Take me there, and I will follow You. By faith, I say, "I'm ready!"

Listen to this worship song via YouTube: "Ready or Not" by Hillsong United

Leslie's Story

Three years ago, my heart had been out of rhythm causing AFib and AFlutter intermittently. It would occur out of nowhere leaving me scared and helpless. I found a great doctor and had two procedures to surgically rewire my heart, but I begged the Lord for the *why.*

I told Him, "I'm too young, too active, too healthy. I don't belong with the gray hairs in the cardiac unit." Even my cardiologist said, "What's a nice girl like you doing in a place like this?" I began earnestly and diligently seeking the Lord and begging for answers. He revealed that He needed to rewire *my* heart so it could align with *His* heart.

Now He has invited me to a spacious place full of treasures filled with wonder, hope, and expectancy. During this first devotional day, I felt like I was on a mountain top with my arms wide open, hands up in surrender giving my *all* to the All in All.

Just knowing that Jesus *"reveals deep and hidden things"*[1] ignites my soul. It steadies me and positions me for a month of surrender and trust. I am expecting *big* things from my Savior. But I must be available to receive His treasures as I sit, study, and *engage* with Him daily. I truly believe that if we are committed to God, He will commission us to expansion and favor in our territories. I long for this intimacy and a road of wonder. I am ready to fall deep into His lavished *"life of love"*[2] for me.

Have you been in the wilderness, wandering aimlessly, or in a long time of waiting? Then come with us on an adventure with the Most High, the Almighty, the One who adores you and longs to go deep into the desires of your heart. Are you ready?

Reflections

DAY

2

YOU CAN HAVE IT ALL

"Broken and weeping, she covered his feet with the tears that fell from her face. She kept crying and drying his feet with her long hair. Over and over she kissed Jesus' feet. Then she opened her flask and anointed his feet with her costly perfume as an act of worship."
-Luke 7:38, TPT

The very thing that was most costly to this woman was poured out on the feet of Jesus. The very thing that held the most worth to her, probably worn around her neck, was broken and emptied on His precious feet. She was probably undone by the love and acceptance of Jesus. She was probably undone by simply being near Him. Her tears may have been an expression of longing for freedom and healing, but in the presence of Jesus, her anointing of His feet turned her longing into worship. Freedom was on its way.

She didn't need to maintain her dignity; she just needed to pour it out on His feet. It wasn't a waste to her. Perhaps a sacrifice, but never a waste.

This is a time of great invitation to intimacy with Jesus. Today, He is wooing you. Your passions get to be enwrapped in His heart, completely overwhelmed by the love of the Father. It's a time Jesus is calling His Bride into a radical, fiery, faith-filled, supernatural, all-consuming love for the Bridegroom.

Our whole lives poured out at His feet. He takes us up, wraps us in Himself, and sets our hearts ablaze. It's our hour of greatest intimacy with Him.

I believe the Lord desires for us to hear:

> You will see and experience deeper levels of who I Am. Don't resist. Don't fear. I Am good, and I Am safe. You can dare to go where you've never gone before. It will be all-consuming, and the things of the world - pursuits, fame, acceptance, reputation - will begin to fall away. I will consume all of it with who I Am. And you will worship Me in this place. New levels of worship I Am taking you to, right now. Do you feel your heart burning inside of you? That's Me. I Am melting away the things that don't need to remain any longer. I will take as much as you are willing to give. I Am coming in fire and fury, coming after My Bride. I paid My life for her. I Am releasing a tidal wave of My exorbitant love that will completely consume you. And you will live and find life in this place … this place of worship at My feet.

Listen to this worship song via YouTube: "Alibaster Heart" by Kalley Heiligenthal and Bethel Music

Katlyn's Story

In today's devotional, I am encouraged by the reminder that freedom is on its way.

I have struggled with anxiety for most of my life, but in the last couple of months it has escalated to a point that some days it is crippling. A day without panic is a victory for me, but each day is a battle. I feel God telling me that this year will be one of freedom, and I am trusting Him with that.

Much like the woman who anointed Jesus' feet, I will come before Him bringing all I have. As I worship, He will burn away the things inside me that don't need to remain any longer. He paid His life for me, and at His feet I find life.

Reflections

DAY

3

Drawing into His Heart

"But Mary treasured up all these things and pondered them in her heart."
-Luke 2:19

"But his mother treasured all these things in her heart."
-Luke 2:51b

Before Mary had the complete picture, her treasuring process had already begun. She became captivated and pondered the marvel of God right before her very eyes. She didn't seem to try to figure it out. All she had was the word of promise spoken to her. But she had to walk it out.

Mary had to choose to believe, by faith, that God was true and that His Word was trustworthy. She had to walk out the promise. And the declaration of her life would be, *"Nothing is impossible with God."*[3] I believe that the very fibers of Mary's heart were being changed as she chose to believe God at the very beginning of her story.

As I sat with the Lord, He placed this hope on my heart for you:

> A story is being declared right now that is being birthed inside of you. It is indeed originating in an invitation to intimacy with Me and partnership with My purposes. Academia is good, but an encounter with Me is better.
>
> What is being released throughout the earth is an invitation, "Come with Me." I have things to show My precious people, and I have places I want to take them. We are going to move in step together to accomplish what is on My heart. It will be the most glorious dance of partnership. I will lead, and you will follow in step, My beautiful Bride. It's not time for hesitation, analyzation, or procrastination. The time is now.
>
> I will restore life to the desert places in your heart; My river will run through barrenness. The goodness of My promises spoken to you in My Word will be fulfilled. They will overflow with the delights of My Kingdom. Those who believe will see. Those who are hungry for Me will feast. I've set a banquet table before My people right now. Whoever longs to come and dine with Me will truly be full of all I have prepared for them. I've said it over and over to you, these are the days of expectant joy, and My grace will take you there. My favor will cause you to remain there. My faithfulness will establish what is born out of our intimacy and union together.

Let this prayer, "Lord I want Your heart," become the prayer of your 31 days. He will be faithful to answer it; I promise.

Listen to this worship song via YouTube: "Closer" Bethel Live with Lyrics

Stacy's Story

I have known and followed Jesus for 21 years and have often heard people talk about how they were "in love" with Him. What did that mean? I thought it should be evident that I loved Him by how I did my Bible studies, mentioned God in a conversation with others, or served in several ministries at my church. But I didn't feel "in love" with Him. Was it even possible to "love" someone you couldn't see, couldn't hug, or couldn't audibly hear?

On a mission trip to Latin America, I sat in what seemed to be the 100th one-room house of utter poverty with dirt floors and toilets without seats. The Latin American woman was so gracious, kissing us on both cheeks, finding chairs from another room, and insisting that we sit for our visit.

As I listened to my interpreter share the gospel and honed into the depravity of life without Jesus, I began to withdraw from the conversation, aware of the presence of Jesus. I began to reflect on how much Jesus has done for me; how much He cares for me; how much He has done for everyone; how much He cares for everyone. And like my salvation moment, I was overwhelmed with something I had not felt before. I had this unexplainable sense of joy and wasn't sure what it was all about.

I fell in love with Jesus!

Reflections

DAY

4

THIS MOMENT RIGHT NOW

"Joining them at the table for supper, he took bread and blessed it and broke it, then he gave it to them. All at once their eyes were opened and they realized it was Jesus! Then suddenly, in a flash, Jesus vanished from before their eyes! Stunned, they looked at each other and said, 'Why didn't we recognize it was him? Didn't our hearts burn with the flames of holy passion while we walked beside him? He unveiled for us such profound revelation from the Scriptures.'"
-Luke 24:30-32 TPT

The very presence and words of Jesus caused the disciples hearts to burn within them. There was just something about that Man. They felt it, and none of them knew that until He was gone. Their flaming hearts created a fellowship around this reality. Together, their hearts burned for Jesus. They would need this common love for Jesus for what was about to be born through their very lives.

The Church was about to be born, and the flames of fire that resided in their hearts would rest on their heads.

They certainly could have stayed paralyzed in the loss of their Savior, but instead they went with the revelation they had seen and known and went to tell the good news to the other disciples. They had something inside of them burning to get out. Jeremiah spoke of this same thing when he said, "*[H]is word is in my heart like a fire, a fire shut up in my bones. I am weary of holding it in; indeed, I cannot.*" [4]

This is the hour that the Bridegroom is longing for His Bride to burn with passion for Him. We are not to stay paralyzed in fear or trepidation, but we are to run with the declaration of their testimony.

I believe the Lord desires us to hear:

> I Am drawing women who have a passion to bring Jesus His inheritance: the nations. They will be global landscape-envisioned women. They will not be bound by small thinking or building their own kingdoms. They will have a heart to see women in all nations and from all demographics set free and liberated by the gospel as heirs of the promise - total liberation because of the cross. They will be a worshiping group who long for My presence first and foremost. It is in this place of intimacy that I will establish a Kingdom-building team of wonder women who believe Me for even greater things. It will not be about age or experience but solely on hunger and vision.

Let's live this life asking Him to let our hearts burn with a passion for Jesus like we have never known.

Listen to this worship song via YouTube: "Endless Alleluia" by Lizzy King

Shirin's Story

Passion, intensity, heart-felt, freedom, and truth are words that I resonate with at the core of my existence. I crave the "deep unto deep" places of complete honesty and transparency - with my community and with my relationship with the Lord. These are the kinds of relationships that cost everything. The disciples knew that they were literally signing their death certificates by choosing to follow Jesus. Oh, to live in this place of complete surrender, dependency, and wonder. To lose it all to gain Him.

I've had the privilege to live in the midst of some of the bravest people on earth. I grew up in Iran before the revolution, being forced to leave in 1979 when a radical Islamic regime promised the country greater freedom. This beautiful country has subsequently been ravaged by the lies of Islam. However, the Lord will, and is, having the final say. Iran and its Persian people are falling in love with Jesus in such tangible and real ways. Thousands upon thousands have chosen to follow Jesus in the last decade. Laying everything down - family, jobs, friends, culture, security, and even their homeland - to trust and pursue the Lord. Fire burns in their hearts, and the worship that pours out of them carries the purest sound. My heart longs and beats for this kind of authenticity. My heart-felt message to you is that we, too, in the West can burn with this kind of passion for Jesus.

This is our moment right now, our right as His daughters. It is ours for the taking. This devotional passage on "Wonder" refreshed me to the core. It contains keys to freedom and transformation. It reminded me of the wonders Jesus has waiting for us right now as we look to Him.

1 Corinthians 2:9 in The Passion Translation puts it this way: *"Things never discovered or heard of before, things beyond our ability to imagine - these are the many things God has in store for all His lovers."*

Let's pursue Him with heart-felt passion, intensity, freedom, and truth.

Reflections

DAY 5

HERE COMES THE FIRE

"[A]nd I will call on the name of the Lord. The God who answers by fire - he is God."
-1 Kings 18:24b

There is so much to feast on in this story from 1 Kings 18. Elijah had a promise from God. In a land of severe drought, God was going to send rain. Elijah stuffed the promise in his belt and was about to walk through the greatest test of faith that his life depended on. The Lord called Elijah to put Him on display, which could have cost Elijah everything. God showed up and ignited an altar filled with water - the most precious commodity of that day. In fact, it was an altar overflowing with water. Fire came down and consumed the altar and all the water. That symbolic "heart" of worship had to be ignited and consumed.

What is in your heart regarding the promise of God? What do you know that, as most true to you, God has spoken in the secret place? You, like Elijah, may find yourself pouring out faith that doesn't make rational sense, but God has commanded you to fill that altar until it's overflowing with water because He wants to ignite it with His power and goodness and faithfulness and presence. The insanity of faith becomes worship that releases the fulfillment of the promise.

We will talk about the fulfillment of the promise on Day 6, but first things first: the altar of your heart. Is it crying out for God to take that very sacrifice and set it ablaze? He's coming to ignite our lives with a fire of passion like we have never experienced if we will simply give Him permission.

I believe the Lord desires for us to hear:

> I desire to ignite a fire in My people. To those willing to climb upon the altar of sacrifice to the Lord, I will ignite with a flame of fire. I will consume My people, whatever they are willing to give Me. Even if it's just a moment or an inch or if it's all of them, I will come and consume. I will overtake. I will overshadow. I will make My power and goodness known in dimensions they have never seen, never experienced. Dimensions of My love and power to be felt and grasped and experienced. New depths. New heights. Valleys of worship and peak exploits into My heart. I will come like I promised. I will fill and I will fulfill.
>
> Would you dare to open your hands and give Me the greatest desires and passions and treasures of your life? Would you dare to lay before Me your dreams and treasures? Your plans and expectations? Even your disappointments? I want to come and consume

all of it. I want to make your life an ignition point of My goodness and My glory.

Do you not know I can expand the very things you think you need and desire? Do you know I Am the God of abundance, and these very things were born in My heart for you before the world was created? Your worship of Me. Your encounter of Me. New heights. New depths. New places in Me. Let's go! Are you ready?

Listen to this worship song via YouTube: "Insatiable" by Kim Walker-Smith (Official Lyric Video)

Dedra's Story

The message and song from Day 5 are so powerful. I feel like I've been going through the motions. I've been spiritually numb. I've been struggling to get past physical and emotional abuse from my father and sexual abuse from another man as a teen.

When I told my story as a teen, I was the one blamed. At that point, I knew no one had my back. My home was not a safe place. I learned that everything just needed to appear to be perfect. I needed to be perfect. Thirty years later, I have guilt and shame and fear, and I am broken. I have spent years working in the ministry wearing a mask, not letting people past a certain point.

The song "Insatiable" got me. I'm a singer, so music speaks to me in a way that words cannot. I want it all. I want that fire. I want to lay down all the pain, wounds, and brokenness. I want to surrender everything to Him. I must get past the fear. I've lived with this for so long that I don't know who I am without it. But I know I want to be a better wife for my husband and a better mom for my kids. I've been hiding for too long.

Reflections

DAY

6

BRINGING THE PROMISE

"And Elijah said to Ahab, 'Go, eat and drink, for there is the sound of a heavy rain.' So Ahab went off to eat and drink, but Elijah climbed to the top of Carmel, bent down to the ground and put his face between his knees. 'Go and look toward the sea,' he told his servant. And he went up and looked. 'There is nothing there,' he said. Seven times Elijah said, 'Go back.'

"The seventh time the servant reported, 'A cloud as small as a man's hand is rising from the sea.' So Elijah said, 'Go and tell Ahab, "Hitch up your chariot and go down before the rain stops you."' Meanwhile, the sky grew black with clouds, the wind rose, a heavy rain started falling and Ahab rode off to Jezreel. The power of the Lord came on Elijah and, tucking his cloak into his belt, he ran ahead of Ahab all the way to Jezreel."

-1 Kings 18:41-46

The insanity of faith becomes worship that releases the fulfillment of the promise.

Before Elijah heard the sound of rain, He declared to Ahab rain was coming. Elijah climbed to the top of the mountain and positioned himself in a birthing position. His positioning of his body and heart were not going to move until he saw the fulfillment of the promise. He did not stop expecting. He did not stop looking. He did not stop birthing faith into the promise. On the seventh time of looking, his servant saw a cloud in the distance. That was all he needed to send him running in faith.

You cannot stop believing God on the sixth time of waiting and hoping and praying. God is asking you to remain positioned in intercession for the breakthrough. If you know the word of the Lord in your heart, then you hold on, stay focused, and continue to worship until the promise is fulfilled.

First, the altar of your heart is positioned and then the fire of God falls. Nothing left of this world, but all of you consumed by Him and for Him. Then the fulfillment of the promise is not just for you; it is for the nations and generations.

My prayer for you this morning:

> Fire of God, fall and ignite and consume us. I pray for an anointing of faith today, to believe You for the fulfillment of the promise. But Lord let us focus not on the fulfillment but on the One who gave the promise. Get our eyes and our hearts laser focused on You.
>
> I pray that You take us to the top of the mountain this month and pour out radical faith to see what You see

and expect heaven to fall on our families, cities, nation, and world.

Let us carry the flame of the Holy Spirit every place our feet touch. In the name of Jesus.

Listen to this worship song via YouTube: "Heaven Fall" by Cody Carnes

Patrice's Story

As I entered the 31 days of devotion and fasting, I laid three specific prayers before the Lord. These were not necessarily new prayers, but my focus and intention were now deeper because I wasn't just praying; I was coupling my prayers with fasting.

Immediately I felt oppressed. The more intensely I prayed, the more doubts and frustrations clouded my mind, which led to friction with my husband and children. I asked the Lord, out loud, if all I was put on earth to do was to pray for my family but never see Him show up and answer any of my prayers.

After I laid those feelings before my Father, I read Day 6 about Elijah expecting rain. The Lord opened the eyes of my heart to see the expectation Elijah had even before a cloud formed in the sky. He said, *"...there is the sound of a heavy rain."* [5] The reality was no one heard rain or thunder, because there was not even one cloud. Elijah sent his servant seven different times to look out over the sea to report any clouds. All the while, Elijah *"bent down to the ground and put his face between his knees."*[6] Elijah prayed with fervent expectation because the Lord put a promise in his heart that it would rain. Elijah would not relent until the rain came.

As I read, the Lord rebuked me to quit grumbling about how and when He answers my prayers. I am to position myself like Elijah with humility and expectation that the answer is coming. Breakthrough is coming. Clarity is coming. His promises are coming.

In her writing, Julie said, "God is asking you to remain positioned in intercession for the breakthrough." That is exactly what I did. I stayed in position. I reminded myself over and over to whom I am praying.

The 31 days of fasting has forever reshaped my posture in prayer and revived the biblical call to fasting that is lacking in the American church today. God releases His supernatural power when we pray and fast.

Reflections

DAY

7

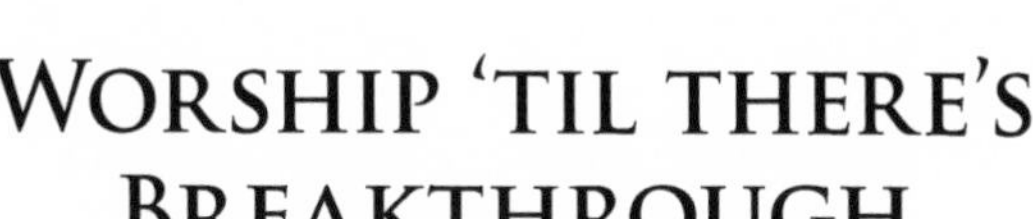

WORSHIP 'TIL THERE'S BREAKTHROUGH

"About midnight Paul and Silas were praying and singing hymns to God, and the other prisoners were listening to them. Suddenly there was such a violent earthquake that the foundations of the prison were shaken. At once all the prison doors flew open, and everyone's chains came loose."
-Acts 16:25-26

Everything about this moment was supernatural.

You cannot sing praise to God if it doesn't already reside in you, especially when faced with the brutality of pain and imprisonment. That's supernatural. Your worship that wells up in brutal circumstances, suffering, heartache, and loss is the supernatural response of what you pull from deep within.

The prisoners and the prison walls heard a new sound, one they had probably never heard. Then, as the atmosphere was saturated with worship, the very ground began to shake. The prison doors opened, and everyone's chains fell off. It was a miraculous moment of supernatural freedom for all those with no possible hope of freedom.

But God.

Worship preceded the breakthrough. Worship and the declaration of praises to the One who could set them free in that moment and for all eternity, is what broke everything loose. And if you read the rest of the story, so many encountered the salvation of Jesus that day.

He sets you free so that others can receive freedom. Oh, the glorious power of the gospel.

As you press into the heart of God this month, are you reading these words longing and praying and believing for a breakthrough? Your greatest position is in worship.

There is a battle for your faith when you wait for breakthrough because if the enemy can rob your belief in the goodness of God, you stop holding on and stop standing in the unwavering, unchanging character of God. Your worship must get louder and your declarations stronger, even with tears streaming down your face. Don't move from your place of worship until the ground shakes, the doors open, and the chains fall off. Worship is your victory, and the Victor deserves it all.

I believe this is Jesus' heart and hope for us today:

> Daughters of Mine, many of you have lamented the pain of unanswered prayers. Many have held on to the breakthrough through the night and at dawn, but it still has not arrived. Am I not faithful and true? Am I not the one who promised an everlasting covenant of My goodness to you? I need you to remain today,

with your gaze set on Me. Let your worship of Me get louder. Let conviction rise in you today as I anoint you to an even greater faith to trust and follow Me. I will be faithful and true to you to the very end. You do not need to doubt or flounder or question. Just remain with Me a little while. Linger here in worship. I will come and reveal all that is in My heart for you in these days of waiting and worshiping. You will see the hand and power of the Lord to rescue and save and heal and restore, because that is who I Am!

Listen to this worship song via YouTube: "Praise Before My Breakthrough" by Bryan and Katie Torwalt

Janie's Story

I am a 63-year-old, Spirit-filled woman of God.

I often speak this out loud to remind myself who God designed me to be. And it reminds me of who I'm not when the enemy speaks lies to my heart. Power, strength, and confidence rise in me when I speak it. I claim my age in the statement because I have earned wisdom and battle scars. Jesus in me will always be greater than anything Satan throws at me. I choose to boast about that.

If/when I get discouraged, I increase my worship, using it as a weapon. I can't hear Satan's lies when I'm singing loudly about my Jesus or inviting Holy Spirit to come. My heart and face cannot be downcast when my supernatural God is the subject of my worship. Love, joy, and peace flood my soul.

So, worship, my friends. Worship like David did when he danced before the Lord with all his might.[7] Worship and watch the enemy fade away.

"With your help I can advance against a troop;
With my God I can scale a wall."
-Psalm 18:29

Reflections

Come Back to Me

"But I have this against you: you have abandoned the passionate love you had for me at the beginning."
-Revelation 2:4, TPT

I remember a season of my walk with Jesus when I did all the "right things" without the fire and passion I once had for my Jesus. He gently and mercifully took me to this Scripture and invited me to come back to the love and intimacy I had known before busyness and the cares of the world choked it out. His hands and arms were wide open to me. They weren't crossed in disapproval.

So many of us picture the Lord sitting in a swivel chair waiting to turn His back on us in disappointment. He doesn't do that. His disappointment was paid for on the cross.

There's nothing but unwavering love for us; a love that knows no disapproval or disappointment. It's a wooing love. It's a relentless love. And, today, it's an invitation to a new journey into His heart. This is the month you have consecrated before Him. It's a month of honesty and revelation.

Are there places of expectation you have of Him that overshadow your love for Him? Any disappointment? Addiction to busyness? Is there another relationship that is becoming a place of worship where you need to bring to Him?

I invite you to go there with Him in honesty; He already knows. There's no condemnation for those in Christ Jesus.[8] Let Him woo you to a face-to-face discussion, and let Him pour into you the passionate love you once had. This is a chance for the believer. You can reawaken to the love you found when you first believed. That's what He's doing with and in and through His Bride right now. It's your bridal preparation season with Jesus.

I believe God desires you to know this today:

> Oh, that My people would know the abundance of all I not only have for them, but of how I desire to be to them. They search and search for the things of this world to fulfill the only place I can fill. Oh, that My people would be marked by the abundance of who I Am. If people would only take Me at My Word. I withhold nothing of My goodness. Everything I have is yours. It all belongs to you. This is your rightful and legal inheritance in My Kingdom. This is rightfully yours, daughter. And nothing will take that away. Nothing will remove this from you. You are My daughter, and if you ask for it - ask for My impossibility - I will do it.

Pray and believe out of the abundance of My Kingdom. Pray and expect as a daughter. There is no fear when you approach Me. There's no such thing as earning My favor. You already have it, simply because the favor of being My daughter is your identity and position. You don't even fathom the royalty and opportunity of this divine adoption. But I Am going to show you. You are going to see My lavish goodness released on you. Position yourself in the truth and in a place of belief where you ponder and treasure. Open your heart to Me today and let Me have it all.

Listen to this worship song via YouTube: "Nothing Else" by The Belonging Co and Cody Carnes

Judy's Story

I was born into a chaotic, alcoholic, broken family, and raised in a faith tradition that focused more on religious rituals and superstition than on a personal relationship with Jesus Christ. I spent my 20s chasing a career and hoping to meet a great man. I was a chronic "fixer" of broken men, hoping to change them so I could be loved. After finally ending a long-term, emotionally abusive relationship, I asked the Lord to forgive me and save me from the mess I called my life. He set me on a lifetime path of returning to Him through learning Scripture and growing in relationship with Jesus.

At the time of this writing I am 62 years old. I have learned that God was with me through all the stages of my life: growing up in a broken, dysfunctional family; the isolating despair of infertility and gut-wrenching miscarriages; the death of family members and dear friends; the joys and sorrows of raising three children; and loving the same, wonderful man for almost 30 years. I can declare, without hesitation, God is my Sustainer, my Refuge, my very present Help in times of sorrow and need.

My life verse has become:

"And we know that in all things God works for the good of those who love him, who have been called according to his purpose."

-Romans 8:28

God uses my pain and suffering to soften my heart toward those who suffer. I have a passion for serving the Lord through my church and a local homeless ministry where I manage the food pantry and oversee various events.

Through the pain and loss, I learned faith. I trust in the Lord for my eternal and present-day salvation. While I may question the twists and turns in the journey, I trust in Him. I have learned to embrace suffering by faith, for He will redeem it for my highest good. The One I need most is always a whispered prayer away.

Reflections

DAY

9

Just One Look

"She said to herself, 'If I only touch his cloak, I will be healed.' Jesus turned and saw her. 'Take heart, daughter,' he said, 'your faith has healed you.' And the woman was healed at that moment."
-Matthew 9:21-22

In a moment, the faith of this woman collided with the compassion of Jesus, and the power for her healing was released. He saw her in a crowd of people. She had been shamed and ridiculed for the duration of her affliction, an outcast for 12 years who was immediately set free.

I love that Jesus simply turned and saw her. He looked at her and literally everything changed. In front of everyone, He honored her with a title we never see Jesus give to anyone else: daughter.

Her life, her identity, her body, her shame, her embarrassment, her disease, her rejection changed in just one moment - just because Jesus looked at her and responded to the faith that was welling up inside of her. All because of a longing for a touch from Jesus, her very life was set free.

We know this biblical reality from the moment we came to know Jesus. Literally, everything changed for us for all of eternity. But He didn't only die so we would know freedom and healing and restoration and hope once we get to heaven. He died so that these very things would be our reality today. He died so this very reality would be born through our lives as we encounter those who desperately need to know Jesus.

More than 3 billion people have yet to hear His precious name. That means 3 billion need the salvation and hope and healing and freedom of Jesus today.

As we move through this month, I want to remind you of this ever-present reality, so you can begin to ask Jesus what He is asking of you. I want to encourage you to ask Him if He has assignments or nations that He wants you to carry in your heart.

Is there an increase of gifting He wants to anoint in your life for this next season? Is there a mantle of increased authority He wants you to walk in for His name's sake? Will you ask Him for your calling to intercession for whatever He is birthing in your spirit?

We want to see those He sees. We want to be transformed by what Jesus sees. We bring the answer to a world dying for an encounter with the Living Christ.

With hands outstretched, ask Him to speak into the above questions and write down what He says to you.

Lord, today, I need You to see the places of my life that need a touch from Jesus. But I also want to be a vessel of the power and goodness of God to others. I pray that You would anoint my life with new vision and purpose. Speak to me. I position my heart to hear You today. In Jesus' name.

Listen to this worship song via YouTube: "Most Beautiful / So in Love" by Maverick City Music and Chandler Moore

Annie's Story

Moving away from home was one of the most challenging and growing experiences of my life. For 18 years, I lived under the comforts and safety of familiarity and family. Then one day I packed up my life and moved to college. I cried myself to sleep the first two weeks because I was sad this change had come. My life at home was good, safe, and I had everything I needed.

For a while, I hated college. I woke up every morning asking, "God, why am I here? Why would You do this to me?" I sank deeper into a sadness I couldn't control. I felt so alone, like it was me against the world.

One Sunday at church, I cried out to God to show me a glimpse of what He was doing. The pastor talked about the vision of the church and what he saw for the city. He said, "No matter where you are, if you just hold on to Jesus, He will transform your life." A wave of peace rushed over me. I was there, not to be alone in a new place, but because Jesus needed me to be there. I was to be a light shining for Jesus to my new friends, into my classrooms, and throughout the entire campus. It was time to wipe away my tears and focus on His Kingdom. After church, I sat in my car and praised Jesus saying, "Lord, I give You my hands; use them, and help me trust You these next four years."

I am part of God's bigger plan. I just couldn't wrap my head around it. Even though there were still moments of doubt, I knew I was where I was supposed to be, and for the first time, I felt excited.

Reflections

DAY

10

I Want to See

"Jesus replied, 'What is impossible with man is possible with God.'"
-Luke 18:27

"Jesus stopped and ordered the man to be brought to him. When he came near, Jesus asked him, 'What do you want me to do for you?' 'Lord, I want to see,' he replied. Jesus said to him, 'Receive your sight; your faith has healed you.' Immediately he received his sight and followed Jesus, praising God. When all the people saw it, they also praised God."
-Luke 18:40-43

The Lord is all about impossibility. It's who He is and what He does.

Today, cry out to Him, "Lord, I want to see You move in impossibility. I don't want my faith to remain in what I think is possible or what I have seen before or what I can imagine. I want to see the supernatural at whole new levels. I pray for a deposit of radical faith to find You, Jesus, in a space I haven't seen before. I don't want to sit on the roadside, begging and waiting. I want to be right in the middle of all You are doing throughout the earth. Lord, I want to see. I want to see prophetically. I want to see for my family, my work, my ministry.

I want to see You walk through the deep recesses and spaces and moments of my life. I want to see You alive and active. Open my eyes to see You today."

I believe the Holy Spirit desires for us to hear these words:

> The man sat begging because everyone had abandoned him. He had to beg to survive. My daughters don't need to beg, nor do they need to sit along the roadside and wait for Me to pass by. I need them to know the access they have to Me as daughters, not beggars or orphans. All of Me is accessible to them. I long that they would come to Me, believing I Am for them. I think that many are afraid of being disappointed or afraid that I will not answer them the way their hearts desire. And I say, "Trust Me."
>
> Come to Me and let Me give you new eyes to see. I want to pour out revival on the hearts of My daughters. I want them to really see Me for who I Am. I want to give them keen insight and sharpened hearing. Some have become unaccustomed to My voice. I will help them hear Me in this new season. I Am using these 31 days to spark desire for Me. I will fill vats with new oil and anoint My daughters in the secret place for a longing for their Bridegroom. I Am doing it, so receive it now.

Listen to this worship song via YouTube: "God I Look to You" by Bethany Wohrle

Lisa's Story

The Lord is all about impossibility. *Name Above All Names* is my special name for God – the unknown name that has not been defiled. The Lord has shown me this name is above all that can be named. This *Name Above All Names* is above all cancer, all divorce, all bankruptcy, all fear. It's also the name above all good things like homes, vacations, cars. He is greater than all we could ever seek. He is the Lord of all, Name above all, King of Kings, the Supreme God Head.

May all that is in me praise Your Name, oh Lord. Let Your peace reign over me in all situations.

> Lord, You are above all cancer.
> Lord, You are above all epilepsy.
> Lord, You are above all families.
> Lord, You are above all that can be named.

Lord, I can trust You no matter the storm. I can entrust to You my whole heart and mind and lean on Your understanding which is much more infinite than my own.

Reflections

DAY 11

THE FLAMMABLE ONES

"On the day Pentecost was being fulfilled, all the disciples were gathered in one place. Suddenly they heard the sound of a violent blast of wind rushing into the house from out of the heavenly realm. The roar of the wind was so overpowering it was all anyone could bear! Then all at once a pillar of fire appeared before their eyes. It separated into tongues of fire that engulfed each one of them. They were all filled and equipped with the Holy Spirit and were inspired to speak in tongues - empowered by the Spirit to speak in languages they had never learned."
-Acts 2:1-4, TPT

Pentecost was also known as the Feast of Harvest, which is so perfect for the birth of the church. It was a defining moment for these believers and the marker for all of history. These "flammable ones" were set on fire and sent out to take the world by storm with the powerful demonstration and proclamation of the gospel.

There they were in the upper room, sharing together in their waiting, expectation, obedience, prayer, and passion. Suddenly, a rushing wind filled the whole house. The translation of the word "wind" is the same word as the Spirit. The Holy Spirit came with a roar and what followed was powerful. Suddenly, God moved. They could hear Him, but they couldn't see Him. Suddenly, life looked quite different for this infant church.

Tongues of fire rested on each one. The idea behind fire is purification. A refiner will use fire to purify an object and burn away what is not necessary. This moment was both an infilling and a purification.

> As David Guzik says, "The experience of the followers of Jesus on Pentecost is another example of God sending fire from heaven to show His pleasure and power, but this time, it descended upon living sacrifices (Romans 12:1)."

This is in contrast to sacrifices made in the Old Testament that God would light with His own fire; sacrifices which had already been slain.

These hungry ones were ready. The Lord said to me, "That's because they were My flammable ones." They were ready to be ignited and set ablaze for His glory and purposes. They had nothing better than to wait for Him to come and fill them with power and send them forth. He is longing to find us with the same passion and priorities.

Today the Spirit resides in us and desires to rest upon us.

Ask yourself these questions: Does my life attract the presence of God? Am I one He looks at to find His resting place? Does my life have room for Him to come and sit and remain upon?

Below is my prayer for you:

> Lord, I thank You for the example of those who were waiting for their refining and their empowering. Thank You for dwelling in us with Your Spirit.
>
> I pray that the life of the one reading these words would be a magnet for Your presence. Come and rest on her like You did in the upper room or when You hovered over the empty space in Genesis and spoke life into being.
>
> I pray for a fresh anointing of calling and power for all You have for her in this season, in Jesus name! You are roaring from heaven on behalf of Your precious church. Set her free to run, ablaze with the fire of God.
>
> Speak now, breath of God, into the places that need insight, revelation, and new life for the one reading these words.

Listen to this worship song via YouTube: "Refiner" by Maverick City Music, featuring Chandler Moore and Stefany Gretzinger

Sue's Story

I have lived 60 years and never shared the gospel. Not a statement I like to declare, though true. Also true, I have lived most of my Christian life in the margins. I had an attitude that God couldn't use me, I was too broken, not smart enough, or studied enough.

Last year, God told me to step out in faith and He would meet me. I decided to join a mission trip. On the trip, I experienced a surrendering and empowering of the Holy Spirit - God working through me, His words, His passion, and His love burning within me for those He loves around the world.

In today's devotional, Julie wrote of the Pentecost, the Feast of Harvest, and the "flammable ones." As I read these words, I realized I had become a *flammable one*. I'm ready to be ignited and set ablaze for His glory and purposes. I'm ready and expecting God to tell me where to go, and who to speak to. Looking through His eyes, and asking, "Which direction, Lord?" No longer on the sidelines, entering my empty nesting, retirement years. Excited to find others at my same stage of life to join me and enter into the harvest. Now understanding that the Great Commission was for me, all of us, not just a select few.

"Then Jesus came close to them and said, 'All the authority of the universe has been given to me. Now go in my authority and make disciples of all nations, baptizing them in the name of the Father, the Son, and the Holy Spirit. And teach them to faithfully follow all that I have commanded you. And never forget that I am with you every day, even to the completion of this age.'"

-Matthew 28:18-20, TPT

Reflections

DAY

12

REVIVAL AND ROMANCE

"Therefore I am now going to allure her; I will lead her into the wilderness and speak tenderly to her. There I will give her back her vineyards and will make the Valley of Achor a door of hope. There she will respond as in the days of her youth, as in the day she came up out of Egypt. 'In that day,' declares the Lord, 'you will call me "my husband"; you will no longer call me "my master". I will remove the names of the Baals from her lips; no longer will their names be invoked.'"

"I will betroth you to me forever; I will betroth you in righteousness and justice, in love and compassion. I will betroth you in faithfulness, and you will acknowledge the Lord.

"'In that day I will respond,' declares the Lord - 'I will respond to the skies, and they will respond to the earth; and the earth will respond to the grain, the new wine and the olive oil, and they will respond to Jezreel. I will plant her for myself in the land; I will show my love to the one I called "Not my loved one." I will say to those called "Not my people," "You are my people"; and they will say, "You are my God."'"

-Hosea 2:14-17, 19-23

This is a season of great romance and revival for the Bride of Christ. She is being awakened from her slumber and her wooing from the world. She is beginning to set her affections on the One who is pursuing her with reckless abandon. Jesus already gave everything for her. She's just beginning to realize it. "Like Christ loved the church" is becoming her ever present reality. It's like she's waking up for the first time.

I believe the Lord desires us to know:

> I Am calling and pulling her into Myself in this distinctive dance of affection and love and tenderness. This is so I can breathe into her lungs, placing all My affections upon her, restoring and healing her. I will tell what I believe about her and what heaven says about her.

This is an intimate season. The word "season" indicates the beginning and end of a period of time. But there is no end to this, just the dawning of a new era of divine intimacy and romance between Jesus and His Bride.

New affections will be found. Things that held His Bride down will be broken off. She must be free to receive a new revelation of His love for her and to love Him in return with a love she has yet discovered. Your experience of the love of Jesus is going places you have not yet traversed. I declare it to you, in Jesus name.

"The Spirit and the bride say, 'Come!'"
-Revelation 22:17a

He is putting a "maranatha" on your lips. You are going to long for His coming at a new depth of worship. These 31 days on the mountain with Jesus will change you. You will see Him transfigured before your very eyes. He will give you new eyes and new ears to see and to hear. New oil. New wine.

If you have time to read Hosea, it is a beautiful love story.

I believe the Lord desires us to hear:

> My Bride is awakening. She's coming to life. She won't be like Gomer anymore. She will be devoted to Me and Me alone. Job pursuits are going to change. Entertainment preferences will begin to change. She will have an appetite for Me alone; nothing else will suffice. I'm going to change her pallet for what she tolerates. New pursuits that matter for eternity are being released. Her life trajectory will shift and re-direct. Her cravings will begin to change.
>
> And those tears of pain? I'm wiping them. She will sing and dance again. Laughter will return.[9] The places of affliction will diminish because she will see My right hand of deliverance. There will be a deposit of grit and perseverance to run to the finish line. I will begin to change what she perceives as earthly reward and set eternity in her heart and on her mind. She will begin to live for this. I Am setting My affections upon My Bride and wooing her unto Myself.
>
> Just receive My love. Don't dismiss it or question it. Let Me love you and reveal the depth of what this means to Me today. You need to hear this today. You

need to see this today. Look and listen. Hear the voice of your Bridegroom.

Listen to this Worship song via YouTube: "Extravagant" lyric video by Steffany Gretzinger and Amanda Cook

Lauren's Story

I have battled anxieties throughout life, and as a young adult, my anxiety turned to a major depression. I felt it throughout my body with physical pain and weight loss. Counseling and medication helped a little, but not much. For a while, prayer didn't seem to work.

After struggling for 18 months, I was a shell of who I used to be. All I wanted was to feel good, so I began living life for myself apart from God's best for me. When I was ready for my life to change, I said, "*YES*" to what Jesus offers and put effort into my relationship with Him.

I asked Him to fill me with the power of His Spirit so I would no longer focus on myself, the negative, and the lies. I am living proof that Jesus has the power to change. We just need to cry out to Him, take Him at His word, and know that He can set us free from the things that hold us down and try to limit our effectiveness in life and for Him. He is a good God.

Reflections

DAY 13

He is Coming!

"The bride belongs to the bridegroom. The friend who attends the bridegroom waits and listens for him and is full of joy when he hears the bridegroom's voice."
-John 3:29

I remember when I was 6 years old and the Lord spoke to my mom, "I Am coming back, and you are not ready." It was at this very time we saw the salvation of our entire household.

I always share this part of my testimony when I share the gospel. Recently and unexpectedly, my mom texted me a reminder of what God said to her that day. Forty years had passed since she last mentioned that day. About an hour after receiving my mom's text, I read this quote on Instagram:

> "The Lord is calling some to embrace a season of rigorous preparation to prepare others for the greatest transition in history, the return of Jesus." -Mike Bickle

This thought of Jesus' return flashed across my mind twice in just a matter of hours. I knew the Lord was speaking. I took note of the repetition of the theme. For months, my thoughts have been turned and redirected to the reality that Jesus is returning for His Bride. In fact, I think what was once a part of our doctrine is shifting into our main line of sight. I believe it will be something we will each base our lives' pursuits upon.

I remember sitting across from my translator in Asia as she told me that she hopes to give her life for the sake of Christ and that her nation would come to know Jesus. With tears streaming down her face, she said to me, "We only take people with us to heaven - nothing else."

Sisters, there's been a deposit of eternity placed inside us, a tension that this indeed is not our home. And there's a longing placed inside us for the One who anchors our whole lives. Oh, that we would be filled with the passion and longing for Him and all that He has for us.

I pray He gives you a picture of His face. When He looks at you, He is full of total love and approval and affection and joy. One day we will see Him face-to-face. One day we will dine at the wedding feast of the Lamb. It may not be far off. Are you ready?

Today's theme verse jumped off the pages of my Bible when the Lord gave me the vision for this 31-day encounter to listen for the voice of the Bridegroom.

Will it be in our day, in this generation, that we see our coming King? The reality is that He is coming for His Bride. How do our lives reflect our expectation for this day? How are we preparing for this ever-present reality? Lord, are the affections of our hearts set on You? Are our lamps filled with oil like the five wise virgins? [10]

> Lord, I pray that You would take me deeper and deeper into new facets of Your love. Would You change my focus to eternity, that I would count the cost and live for that day? May my life be a radical testimony of those who have been redefined by love. Fill my lamps with oil. And may the words of my mouths and the meditation of my heart be fixed on the One who paid it all for me and who is worthy of my all.

Listen to this worship song via YouTube: "You're Worthy of it All" by Shane and Shane

Listen to this worship song via YouTube: "In Love Again" by Untitled Worship

Kimberly's Story

After praying for days that Jesus would break down the wall separating me and Him, it happened on Day 13. As I continued to pray and worship, I felt His presence. For a while now, I have sensed and heard God say, "Tell your story." Finally, a few months ago, I started writing it. Grudgingly, I wrote four chapters of the painful, traumatic parts of the chaos that ensued the first 30 years of my life. Something didn't feel right; it felt dark and sad.

But today, there was breakthrough. God showed me that the "story" He's asking me to tell is *our* story. My falling head over heels in love with Him. To share with others the beautiful way He redeemed all my pain, every heartbreak, and even the trauma.

For the last 23 years (after the initial 30), I have been sitting on His shoulders with a view like I could never imagine and often find it hard to describe. I have prayed for years that He would show children and loved ones this view. Some call it scales coming off. I prefer to see it as a spectacular view, one of good defeating evil. One of unspeakable joy and peace. Something one must experience because words don't do it justice.

Today, there was breakthrough and today, there is praise.

Reflections

DAY 14

Complete Healing

"As Peter traveled about the country, he went to visit the Lord's people who lived in Lydda. There he found a man named Aeneas, who was paralyzed and had been bedridden for eight years. 'Aeneas,' Peter said to him, 'Jesus Christ heals you. Get up and roll up your mat.' Immediately Aeneas got up. All those who lived in Lydda and Sharon saw him and turned to the Lord."
-Acts 9:32-35

I love how The Passion Translation pens verse 34: *"Aeneas, Jesus the Anointed One instantly and divinely heals you. Now, get up and make your bed."*

"Say to my soul, I am your salvation."
-Psalm 35:3, ESV

The powerful demonstration of God and Peter's proclamation worked in tandem. These two things also work together in our lives when we step into a moment where only God's power can accomplish something.

He shows up in the miraculous. Many see and turn to the Lord. Our lives are a living demonstration and proclamation of the gospel. It's the way He wanted it from the beginning when God allowed Adam to name the things He created. He wants us to partner with Him.

Peter's eyes were turned to a man who needed freedom and healing. For eight years this man suffered. Peter brought him Jesus, declared his healing, and then Aeneas had something to do. He had to take care of his mat, or as it says in The Passion Translation, "make your bed."

That season was done. It was being put to rest.

I feel this weighty burden in my spirit that it's time for those who have seen healing or deliverance from the Lord to get rid of the mat. Don't keep it as a souvenir. Don't linger on it anymore. Don't dust it off and store it for someone else. Take care of your mat.

The Lord longs to bring the second wave of healing to you, the healing of your soul, including your mind, will, and emotions, from this past season of pain.

I believe there are those who are fasting for their healing during this 31-day encounter, and the hand of the Lord is upon you in that. There are some who need breakthrough for freedom in countless areas. It's coming. Do not lose hope! These things will be a demonstration to a watching world of the very power of the Most High God.

What the church deems as "days of old," are our days. Our now. Our "But God" declarations and experiences. The Lord may do it in an instant or send someone to you. I'm praying for this for many of you this month!

Take care of the mat.

I believe the Lord desires for us to hear these words:

> There are some of My people who can't move past the fact that for eight years they suffered. For eight years they have felt like I abandoned them. Even though I have saved and delivered and healed, they keep looking back at the mat, focused on the disappointment. We can't move into this next season until we have the conversation about the "mat". There's disappointment because of the injustice of the suffering. But all along, My goodness and faithfulness never departed from you. Those past seasons and years were preparing you for what is coming. They were preparation for the "more" of what is ahead. I must reveal who I Am in the pain and in the glory. This is the deposit of deep unto deep.
>
> Those eight years of pain will be part of your story for the proclamation of the gospel in your life. The paralysis preceded the miraculous encounter of all I wanted you to experience. Now go. Declare My wonders to a watching world so many will turn to Me.
>
> I Am declaring My goodness over your disappointment. I Am declaring My love over your past seasons of pain. I was right in the middle of them. I took you through them. I will take you through the current ones and the future ones. Nothing separates you from My love ... nothing ever.
>
> Please don't frame your mat and hang it on your wall and allow the enemy to redefine My goodness to you. He will attempt to assault and assail My goodness. He

> wants to shred My character and prove Me unfaithful. I will heal you in body, soul, and spirit. I will be the salvation of your mind, will, and emotions. You will know wholeness and freedom because that is who I Am. As I take care of your healing, you take care of the mat. Let's move forward into this new season declaring My goodness. I Am good and you are loved. Never forget it.

Jesus and Peter met Aenaes one day, and many others encountered Jesus because of Peter's obedience to go out and minister. Daily, there are people near you sitting in pain, paralysis, poverty of spirit, and suffering. Go. Declare the power of Jesus. Let God do His work. Simply step into the moment and pray with the faith and authority He gives.

> "If we will be like Peter, who went through all parts of the country, then we will also find opportunities for the miraculous power of God." -David Guzik

Listen to this worship song via YouTube: "Good and Loved" by Travis Greene and Steffany Gretzinger

Mary's Story

Had this story talked about waiting for the miraculous power of God for any number other than eight years, I would have pushed the word of correction and encouragement aside and justified it as "for someone else."

But after eight years of waiting, of being disappointed with God's answer to my repetitive eight-year prayer, it is time to see the awesome work of God in the way He did answer my prayer and meet my needs. It is time to take care of my mat, to throw it into the Refiner's fire and see how He transforms my heart and life into His plan and purpose for my forward-moving days.

Hindsight reveals how He lifted me to my feet, put me on solid ground, and brought me to a place of wholeness and freedom that I have never known.

I am no longer a slave to the paralysis of waiting and wondering why God chose to answer my prayer in His way. I am to step into the freedom of His answer, to embrace the new life He has given without the oppression and baggage that once held me captive. I am forever humbled and grateful for His love, provision, and direction into this new life of passion and purpose.

Reflections

DAY

15

He is So Good

"'They will be my people, and I will be their God. I will give them singleness of heart and action, so that they will always fear me and that all will go well for them and for their children after them. I will make an everlasting covenant with them: I will never stop doing good to them, and I will inspire them to fear me, so that they will never turn away from me. I will rejoice in doing them good and will assuredly plant them in this land with all my heart and soul.'"

-Jeremiah 32:38-41

We are halfway through this consecrated month of fasting and worship as we press into the heart of God for vision, clarity, breakthrough, and healing amongst many other things. Smack dab in the middle of our journey is this wide-open space of His goodness.

In fact, our covenant-keeping God didn't make a promise for just past or present; it's an everlasting covenant. This means His covenant with us is eternal, never-ending, perpetual, endless. And the beautiful thing about His goodness is that it isn't contingent on our obedience or performance.

He does not withhold His goodness from us, even when we feel least deserving. These are the times He wants to captivate our hearts and overwhelm us with who He is. Quite honestly, my mind doesn't fathom this, but I long to explore the depths of His goodness. And as much as we long to explore, He longs to take us on the treasure hunt of a lifetime.

My first trip to Asia was with an "Extreme Team." These have now become frequent in my life because of the sheer adventure and encounters with Jesus. We walked through jungles and mountain paths, moving from house to house and village to village as we shared the good news about Jesus. Many had never heard His name before. On this trip, I kept engaging with people who didn't care to know Him as Lord. I was so discouraged.

I was sweaty, salty, exhausted, and frustrated. It was day four, and I arrived breathlessly at the doorstep of a little home. The girl we shared with was not interested in Jesus because she followed a god named Nim. The Holy Spirit prompted me to ask her, "If there's anything I can ask for you from my God, what would that be?" She answered quickly, "I need peace."

Well, that was an easy one.

I know when Jesus walks in the room, our Prince of Peace changes the atmosphere. I told her that Jesus was going to come, and she would feel what it was like to feel the peace of God. My teammate, Peggy, and her translator joined us in the room. As we were about to pray, a fragile old lady came and sat down quietly.

We prayed and the peace of God came and filled that house. I looked up and the little old lady had tears running down her cheeks. I knew

God was stirring in her. She was deaf, so what she was sensing was His presence.

I knelt beside her and asked if I could lay hands on her ears. I simply prayed in Jesus name that God would open her ears. And He did. I shared the good news of Jesus with her that day and she said, *"YES,"* to Him. She had lived 85 years without the knowledge of the goodness of God, but here He came in great power. He rescued her and set His everlasting covenant of goodness upon her.

Today I wonder how many will come to know Jesus because of her life.

She was the only person who said *"YES"* to Jesus the entire trip. But that one encounter forever changed her, and it forever changed me. I saw that at the end of me was the vast ocean of the goodness of God. I stepped my feet into the waters by faith, and He showed up in wonder upon wonder.

At this halfway point, I want you to pray for eyes to see and perceive the goodness of God at new depths. It's time to take an even deeper dive.

> Thank You, Lord, for Your eternal covenant of goodness. Thank You for lavishing Your goodness on me. Plant me, Lord, in open spaces of Your goodness. Rain down from an open heaven over me. Let me traverse the depths of Your goodness. What You speak, You confirm with all You do, out of all You are. Give me ears to hear the songs You sing over me. Give

me eyes to see the random, out of the blue gifts You plant throughout my day. Speak to me Your words of goodness and promise and hope. Open my dream life to experience You in the night watches. Thank You for Your outlandish, unstoppable goodness You display even in times of famine and pain. Lord, put a new song on my lips to proclaim the goodness of God. May I take hold of Your goodness and declare it with all that I am. In Jesus' name, Amen.

Listen to this worship song via YouTube: "Goodness of God" by Jenn Johnson

Keely's Story

Why is it that I doubt His goodness? Why do I think it will end or stop when He is done or when I have doubt? Why do I feel "goodness" can only last for so long? I know His promise:

- He has promised to never leave me for forsake me (Deuteronomy 31:6).
- He has promised that He has plans to prosper me and not to harm me, plans that give me hope and a future (Jeremiah 29:11).
- The Lord is good to all; He has compassion on all He has made (Psalm 145:9).
- Every good and perfect gift is from above, coming down from the Father of the heavenly lights, who does not change like shifting shadows (James 1:17).

I put the Lord in a box, and I limit Him. I do this because I can only see so far, and I limit myself. But that is not our God. He can do things above and beyond our wildest dreams (Ephesians 3:20). When I have been confronted that something is over or something isn't working out, I feel the door is closed. That is when God goes above and beyond what I could ask or imagine. The situation can be as simple as a client meeting when I walk away thinking the client will never work with me. But surprisingly, the client signs contract and becomes one of my best clients.

It is my sin that doubts our Lord in His promises. I am continually learning that His promises are true. On the day I accepted Him as Lord and Savior, He made an everlasting covenant with me. He will never stop doing good. All He asks of us is to love Him with all our heart and soul, to lean on Him, to trust Him, to abide in Him, and to allow Him to be who He has promised He is.

Reflections

DAY 16

It's Time to Ascend

"After six days Jesus took with him Peter, James and John the brother of James, and led them up a high mountain by themselves. There he was transfigured before them. His face shone like the sun, and his clothes became as white as the light. Just then there appeared before them Moses and Elijah, talking with Jesus. Peter said to Jesus, 'Lord, it is good for us to be here. If you wish, I will put up three shelters - one for you, one for Moses and one for Elijah.'

"While he was still speaking, a bright cloud covered them, and a voice from the cloud said, 'This is my Son, whom I love; with him I am well pleased. Listen to him!'

"When the disciples heard this, they fell facedown to the ground, terrified. But Jesus came and touched them. 'Get up,' he said. 'Don't be afraid.' When they looked up, they saw no one except Jesus."
-Matthew 17:1-8

We are traversing a 31-day mountain top journey with Jesus. May this season be transformative to our perception, understanding, experience, and belief about who He is.

In these verses, three disciples head onward and upward to see Jesus in His glory. They hear the voice of the Father and have a life-altering, transforming encounter where their very eyes saw something they had never seen. Their hearts received a specific touch from Jesus that day.

I'm praying the very exact things for you during this 31-day encounter.

Everything in this story, from Jesus leading them up the mountain to their facedown moment of worship, pointed and emphasized Him as the central focus. Moses (who represented law) and Elijah (who represented the prophets) were about to be completely fulfilled in Jesus. The Father directed all His attention to His Son and said, "Listen to him!"

From the shekinah cloud of glory to the transfiguration of Jesus to the words of the Father, all things pointed to Jesus. And what is the response of the disciples? They fell facedown.

Everyone left, the glory cloud faded, and when they looked up, they saw only Jesus. Their entire focus was thrust upon Him. Everyone else disappeared. Although Moses and Elijah were great men, the focus remained Jesus. No one compares to Him. Oh, that we would believe this.

Jesus went to them. He initiated the connection. He reached down and touched them with a touch of compassion and intimacy. He tells them to "Arise!" He comes to comfort, call, and commission them. The same word for "transfigured" in this passage is the word "metamorphosis." It's also the same word used when we're told to "be transformed by the renewing of your mind." [11] Our encounters with Jesus should transform our mind and therefore transform our very beings, including our soul, body, and spirit.

It's a complete transformation beginning with what we believe about the One we have encountered. Encountering Jesus changes everything about us.

Just as they went up, they had to come back down with Jesus. This time of encounter would sear in their memory and perhaps this would be one of their most significant metamorphosis moments. It's key that the Father told the guys to "Listen to him!" If hearing from Jesus were not possible, He wouldn't have commanded it.

His sheep, His daughters, hear His voice. It's a promise and an invitation. And they needed this as they went down the mountain, walked through the crucifixion, and received their commissioning for the days and years ahead.

> Lord, I pray for my sister as You have called her to the top of this mountain. Father, speak. Jesus, touch her today with the comfort and commissioning that is in Your heart for her. She wants to see at higher levels of perspective, so open her to revelation and give her the faith to go there with You.
>
> I ask that You let her experience the shekinah glory of Your Presence. May these 31 days of encounter leave her facedown in worship. When she lifts her eyes, may You be the only thing in her line of sight. Renew and transform her mind to truth, so she may walk in freedom and victory. You were the central focus of the disciples' encounter. No one else held equal with You.

And You promise that at the very end, every knee will bow before You, Jesus.

Transform her mind to live with this reality in view. She desires to live for the One who is wooing her to Himself. She wants to taste and see Your goodness for all eternity! I bless my sister with the goodness and glory of God today, in Jesus name.

Listen to this worship song via YouTube: "Highlands (Song of Ascent)" by Hillsong United

Listen to this worship song via YouTube: "Beautiful" by Vineyard Music

Graylene's Story

Through this 31-day devotional journey, I was encouraged to be transformed by what Jesus sees. I asked Him to show me places in my life that need His touch. As I daily set aside time to pursue Jesus, I saw Him guide me in new directions.

He led me to do a sugar fast. Sugar is one of my stumbling blocks, maybe even an idol. Fasting helped unlock doors. My goal for the sugar fast was to increase my devotion to God by intentionally turning to Him and consuming His Word and not relying on my sweet tooth. During the time of fasting, I asked God to specifically show me how to alter my path so I could grow closer to Him. I believe He told me to be bold in telling others how I have been saved and changed.

One thing I know is that a humble attitude honors God. Each morning I awaken with a readiness to worship Him and start my day focusing on His greatness. Through being quiet, worshiping, and listening, I am being transformed.

Reflections

DAY

17

YOU WILL CROSS OVER!

"Later that day, after it grew dark, Jesus said to his disciples, 'Let's cross over to the other side of the lake.' After they had sent the crowd away, they shoved off from shore with him, as he had been teaching from the boat, and there were other boats that sailed with them.

"Suddenly, as they were crossing the lake, a ferocious tempest arose, with violent winds and waves that were crashing into the boat until it was all but swamped. But Jesus was calmly sleeping in the stern, resting on a cushion. So they shook him awake, saying, 'Teacher, don't you even care that we are all about to die!'

"Fully awake, he rebuked the storm and shouted to the sea, 'Hush! Calm down!' All at once the wind stopped howling and the water became perfectly calm. Then he turned to his disciples and said to them, 'Why are you so afraid? Haven't you learned to trust yet?'

"But they were overwhelmed with fear and awe and said to one another, 'Who is this man who has such authority that even the wind and waves obey him?'"
-Mark 4:35-41, TPT

This Scripture starts with Jesus standing in a boat on the sea with people on the shoreline, perhaps with water lapping their sandals. As Jesus spoke to them in parables, the sea was calm. (If you have time, read the whole chapter of Mark 4.)

To His disciples, Jesus shared the secrets of His Kingdom and revealed mysteries that only He knew.[12] To others who didn't have ears to hear, the Holy Spirit created a luring curiosity to whet their appetites for the One who spoke the very words of life.

He said to His disciples, "Whoever has will be given more."[13] Even more revelation would be given. To those who were hungry, He would fill their mouths with good things.

"Open wide your mouth and I will fill it."
-Psalm 81:10b

If you read the parables in Mark 4, you see that the enemy will stop at nothing to steal, destroy, distract, and choke out what God is revealing, planting, cultivating, and purposing in your life.

When the hand of God moves, the enemy rises up.

So, Jesus released an invitation and a promise to His guys. He said, *"Let's cross over to the other side."*[14] Jesus already saw them on the other side of the sea. He knew exactly where they were going because He was ready to take them there.

I remember two personal times of great invitation with the Lord. One of these defining moments happened when I was 6 years old and Jesus invited me to receive Him as my Savior. The other was about 12 years ago. I pictured myself standing on the shoreline of a huge ocean with water lapping my feet. In that moment the Lord asked me, "Would you let Me take you into the depths of who I Am, to experience more of Me than you have yet known?" I knew the very ocean couldn't contain all of who He was and is. But He was calling me to go in over my head. I confessed my fear and plunged in.

Back to today's story.

The enemy entered the scene as the disciples began their journey to "cross over." The storm came. And with it came the disciples' fear and anxiety and doubt. They lost sight of both Jesus and the vision of "crossing over". All they saw was looming death and despair. Jesus knew this wasn't the end of His story, so He slept, full of the peace of heaven. He was quiet, calm, and confident that the purposes of God would be fulfilled in His life and the lives of His disciples.

He "rebuked" the storm, knowing it wasn't from the hand of God. (I think it probably had to do with the miracle of victory and freedom He was about to release upon the demon-possessed man on the other side. The battle always precedes the breakthrough.)

These fishermen, familiar with the sea, were becoming familiar with the Kingdom of God. And just as He promised, "More would be given." He gave them deep roots of faith, quite contrary to what He spoke about in the parable to those who have no root.

I'm reminded that in the midst of our storms, He speaks and brings peace. Our boats will cross over. The storm does not have the final word over our lives. The boat will not sink because He is in the boat.

I believe the Lord desires for us to hear:

> You will cross over. I Am faithful to My promises. Your destiny is not an eternal storm. I made the trees that formed the boat. I created the wind and seas at the command of My voice. The storm may come, and the enemy may try to play his hand, but I have the final word over your life!
>
> If I Am at rest, can you not be as well? If I Am seated, can you not be as well? The storm is but a moment in the scope of your life, but it is in this place that greater faith is born. It is in this place that you hold onto the very anchor of your soul. And all you believe can be tested here.
>
> Am I faithful to My promises? *YES*! Do I have the power at any second to change the course of the wind? *YES!* Will you hold on and believe I Am accomplishing more inside of you in the middle of this sea than when you stood on the shoreline? Could your placement in this boat, on this sea, with these people, and most importantly with Me, be one of the greatest gifts to you as I cross you over to the other side? Will you let Me reveal My presence and power and peace to you? Can you choose to wipe the lenses of your glasses and look for Me? You can see Me, right here, right now.
>
> We are crossing over. We are on the way. You will see Me in ways you have never known except on this sea, in this boat, with these people. So, take heart and worship Me in the middle of this because I Am coming as you asked. The work you permitted Me to do when

you first gave your life to Me, I will faithfully and abundantly complete. That is My promise to you. But I ask you now for your agreement with My heart and My purposes. Fear and doubt need to be silenced as I anchor your life in faith and worship.

Listen to this worship song via YouTube: "Way Maker" by Leeland

Patti's Story

Through this devotional's song, "Way Maker", God reminded me that He is always working, whether I see Him or not, feel Him or not, and that His name is above loneliness, depression, disease, and cancer. I needed to hear these truths in that I am single, getting older, and have health challenges. Each of these can lead to fear and depression if I'm not clinging to, relying on, and trusting in God.

As I worshiped Him, I received His peace and assurance that He is greater than anything the enemy tries to use to discourage me. I know God is doing a tremendous and life-changing work in me, and the enemy wants to choke it out. From Julie's comments, I was encouraged that, like the disciples in the storm, Jesus knows this isn't the end of my story. My boat will cross over, and I will not sink because He is in my boat.

As I look for Him, God reveals more of His presence and power and peace to me, and so I choose to hold on to Him, trusting His goodness, fully surrendered to His will, and excited to be a part of His plans. Thank You, Lord!

Reflections

DAY

18

DAUGHTER OF MINE

"So the young son set off for home. From a long distance away, his father saw him coming, dressed as a beggar, and great compassion swelled up in his heart for his son who was returning home. So the father raced out to meet him. He swept him up in his arms, hugged him dearly, and kissed him over and over with tender love."
-Luke 15:20, TPT

"'My Son,' the father said, 'you are always with me and everything I have is yours.'"
-Luke 15:31

"Drink deeply of the pleasures of this God. Experience for yourself the joyous mercies he gives to all who turn to hide themselves in him. Worship in awe and wonder, all you who've been made holy! For all who fear him will feast with plenty."
-Psalm 34:8-9, TPT

I love the heart of the father in this passage from Luke as he expresses his goodness and acceptance and unconditional love for both sons, the one far off and the one at home. It's His embrace of us today, regardless of our mistakes or disillusionment or experiences. In Psalm 34, David expresses the goodness of the Lord as he escaped the lunacy of Saul and the threat on his life. He had an opportunity to question God, but instead he declared His goodness and abundance.

In 2009, my family experienced the impact of the economy fallout quite personally. I was taking on assignments in ministry that put me on the frontlines where I was exposed to the fiery darts of the enemy. At that point, I didn't know how to battle.

I remember waving my white flag of surrender to the enemy because the cost was overshadowing my faith to worship and keep my sight on Jesus. "Hard" became my new normal for many years. We had to sell our beautiful, spacious home. Friendships were pruned from my life, and I was literally pulled into this place where it was just the Lord and me.

During that season the Lord gave me a dream of Father God driving an old 1967 Chevy with Jesus in the passenger seat. He was huge and could barely fit into the seat. He had a long white beard, and as they pulled up to where I was standing, Jesus got out and ran to me. I will never forget the dream and still smile at the image of my Father behind the wheel of that car. I woke up sobbing because I knew I had just had a significant visitation.

But God!

The things I now write to you came out of that hard and painful season. Nothing will be wasted. I promise. Let me testify like David, we "will feast with plenty."[15]

Sisters, we have a divine opportunity to "run to the Father and fall into grace." He meets us with so much compassion and tenderness.

In a culture that bears so many father wounds, I believe He wants us to know and experience what true Fathering in Him looks like. Pain and suffering take a toll on our theology of a good Father. Receiving abuse and neglect or unwarranted rejection from an earthly dad shifts our belief to only being able to grasp partial understanding of who He really is and the deep, deep love of a good, good Father.

"And he will turn the hearts of the fathers to their children,
and the hearts of the children to their fathers..."
-Malachi 4:6a, ESV

Your Heavenly Dad wants to heal the wounds you carry, and He wants to do it now so that you can live and breathe in fullness. He desires for you to fully understand and experience Him as your Father, Jesus and the Holy Spirit. The Holy Spirit prompted the following words in my spirit for you:

> If only you could see My face of longing for you, these eyes of compassion and these arms of embrace. I want to touch places in your heart that have been kept hidden because they were just too painful to deal with. I understand, and I see, and I know.
>
> In fact, I have stored up all the tears you have wept. I Am going to pour them back out on your life. They are going to be the very water that wets the new ground I Am tilling in your life. And you are going to see a harvest of plenty come forth from this pain. I will restore to you all the enemy has tried to steal, kill, and destroy in your life. My heart as a Father is to embrace

you. That is why I had to send My own Son to come and get you. And right now, My Spirit is wooing you with deep love and passion, stirring up in you a new longing and desire. Old things are gone; a new page is being turned; a new day is dawning. I declare to you *new* life.

Will you just do one thing for Me? Will you place every hurt and wound that comes to mind in your two hands? Will you turn your hands and open them and let Me look at these things with you? And will you let Jesus place His nail-scarred hands right on top of your hands and take these things from you?

I want to place new things in your hands. Ask Me right now what those things are and don't question it. Let Me tell you everything I Am giving you in exchange for the things you just gave to Me. Write them down, ponder them, treasure them, and watch for them. You will see My goodness, My abundance, My healing, My hope, My restoration, My mercy, My love for you like you may have never experienced. It's a new day, precious daughter of mine, and everything I have is yours.

Listen to this worship song via YouTube: "Run to the Father" by Cody Carnes

Anna's Story

The Lord carried me through an extremely difficult year in 2019. In that year, I lost a family member to murder and another to suicide. I was diagnosed with breast cancer. During the last six months of the year, I had three surgeries related to the treatment for breast cancer. I also had an emergency appendectomy in the middle of those three surgeries. I watched my parents lose their retirement savings, our beloved 13-year-old dog had to be put down, and we had an unbelievable car repair costing around $5,000. The blows were continual and staggering. And yet, through it all, God spoke to me so clearly. Even through my tears and heartache, He showed His unending love and mercy.

As I came into January 2020, I was weary and fiercely clinging to Jesus. As I began to pray and fast, I understood how God allowed the soil of my life to be plowed. We can look at the broken "soil" in our lives and see it as broken, or we can look at it and understand it is ready for planting. God was beginning something new in me. To be honest, I don't even know what the new thing is, but I know I can trust the One who carried me through the heartache of 2019.

As I prayed and fasted, God continually spoke the words "abundance" and "blessing" over me. Abundance? Blessing? What I walked through felt like an abundance of heartache and it did not feel like a blessing. Yet over and over, these words came up. In my dreams He said, "Just wait for My blessing. It is going to be so good." Three people in completely unrelated circumstances told me, "The Lord will restore what the locusts have eaten." God told me He was giving me a voice to speak because of the pain I had walked through; a voice to speak of

His goodness. He gave me the verse that says, *"Now then, stand still and see this great thing the Lord is about to do before your eyes* (1 Samuel 12:16)!"

Toward the end of 2019, God gave me a vision of taking a stack of papers and placing it at the base of a towering Sequoia tree. The stack of papers represented all the sorrow from that year; each hard thing was a piece of paper in the stack. God's goodness was the towering, mighty tree. My stack of problems didn't compare to the towering tree. To take my list of things and say that God isn't good because of cancer, death, finances, etc., is to grossly ignore or just not comprehend the magnitude of what God has saved us from through our life in Him.

Nothing can shake my firm knowledge in the goodness of God, even if none of my earthly circumstances ever change. What I know is that I have seen the goodness of the Lord. He has given me joy even in pain. He has pulled me to His heart. He has spoken words over me of healing and love. What I have come to know is that God carries us through hard times and good times. His love doesn't change based on our circumstances.

Reflections

DAY

19

His Voice and Your Voice

"Now the earth was formless and empty, darkness was over the surface of the deep, and the Spirit of God was hovering over the waters. And God said ..."
-Genesis 1:2-3a

"The voice of the Lord echoes through the skies and seas. The Glory-God reigns as he thunders in the clouds. So powerful is his voice, so brilliant and bright, how majestic as he thunders over the great waters!"
-Psalm 29:3-4, TPT

"There's a private place reserved for the lovers of God, where they sit near him and receive the revelation-secrets of his promises."
-Psalm 25:14, TPT

"Then he said to me, prophesy to these bones and say to them, 'Dry bones, hear the word of the Lord! This is what the Sovereign Lord says to these bones: I will make breath enter you, and you will come to life. I will attach tendons to you and make flesh come upon you and cover you with skin; I will put breath in you, and you will come to life. Then you will know that I am the Lord.'"
-Ezekiel 37:4-7

"... and I saw the glory of the God of Israel coming from the east. His voice was like the roar of rushing waters, and the land was radiant with his glory."
-Ezekiel 43:2

When God speaks, things come into existence. When He speaks, life is created, and destinies are born. People are healed. Hope is restored. The blind see and deaf hear. At His voice, the dead are raised to life. He sets planets into motion at His very words. All of life was born on the lips of God. Everything is sustained because He sustains it by His Word. When He speaks, His words matter because they carry a reverberation through eternity outside of space and time. They consume our very present reality.

His voice is not creating possibility; it formulates probability, substance, essence, and life.

In light of that very truth, God enables us, who carry the very presence of Holy Spirit, to declare and decree His word into situations. He allows us to speak life into dead things and to call things to come into God's purposes and His fullness. We have the God-given ability and authority to speak life or death into people and circumstances. [16]

One of my favorite Scripture passages is Ezekiel 37. It's been my manifesto in prayer and the framework for me to see things that are not as if they are. The Lord commanded Ezekiel to "prophesy," to speak the revealed words of God, into old dead bones. If you read the rest of the story, you will see that the bones assemble, and an army arises. God breathes His breath of life into them as Ezekiel prophesies.

Now it's your turn! You have spent the last 18 days pressing into Jesus and letting His Word transform, reveal, and speak to you. He may have given you words, Scriptures, pictures, visions, dreams, and new things stirring in your spirit. They are your treasures and promises you carry.

I believe the Lord also wants you to speak back to Him what you have heard Him say to you in quiet. Begin to speak life to the things He has shown you. Begin to turn God's words back to Him in prayer. Speak to your marriage, your prodigal children, and your loved ones who don't know Jesus. Like Ezekiel did, prophesy to these places and to these people. Command dead things to come to life. This is the beautiful partnership of listening and then activating what you hear from God with faith by letting your words speak life.

If you have a promise from the Lord or a dream God has given you, tell it to come to life. Listen and prophesy just Ezekiel did.

I am loving the book "The Prophetic Voice of God" by Lana Vawser.[17] In it she writes:

"Friends, today I want to encourage you- you have the power to shift atmospheres, decree life, decree encouragement, hope, healing, and freedom wherever you go. Feast upon His Word, study it, meditate on it, engage in it, linger with Him. Ask Him what He is dreaming about, what He is decreeing, what He is seeing, and repeat it.

"Remember, every time you decree, every time you intercede, every time you repeat what He is saying, you are filling the bowls of heaven; you are sowing in the Spirit into what He is doing–into breakthrough, shift and release of His presence and His Kingdom. You are partnering with what He is doing to bring His reality to earth.

"Write out the decrees He is giving you and keep repeating what He is saying. Watch what glorious things He will do. Today could be the day that one decree sees the bowls of heaven tip, and that one decree changes everything."

This is my prayer for you today:

> Lord, I pray that my sister will have Your words in her heart and on her lips. May she boldly declare what You are saying over all the people and things You have assigned to her. Give her vision and language to pray bigger than her mind can articulate. And give her faith as she waits for the victory.

Listen to this worship song via YouTube: "I'm Listening" by Chris McClarney (featuring Hollyn)

Veronica's Story

Decreeing God's Word is powerful. It can change the lives of His people. It certainly changed mine.

In 2014, I was diagnosed with Lyme Disease, which was believed to have been contracted 18 years earlier. The symptoms were joint pain, depression, brain fog, severe headaches, vertigo, skin irritations, and muscle pain. I was in bed for a minimum of two days a week from pain. Miserable and totally depressed, I removed myself from every group and leadership role.

Thankfully, my Lord and Savior met me right where I was. Over the next three years He and I interacted via His Word. One day when I was praying God's Word, I remember saying, "But God, these prayers are not true for me." At that moment the verse Romans 4:17 came to mind. While I had read that verse before, the part where it says that God can call into being things that don't yet exist was something I had never seen before.

"Father, are You saying to pray Your Word as though it was my truth?" A cautious hope came over me as I thought, "This is what my Father wants me to do." Every day I spoke life via God's Word out loud. Since the enemy cannot hear our thoughts, I wanted to make sure he heard the verses I spoke.

Then the Lord took me to John 5:1-8. When He asked the invalid, "Do you want to be well?" I stopped reading. I could envision Jesus standing before me, looking me directly in the eyes, asking me that question! Then it hit me that I had been sick for so long I had no idea what it was like to be well. I yelled out loud, "Yes, Jesus! I want to be well." Then more quietly, "Jesus, help me know how to be well. Show me the way and I will walk in it." Then I fell over in a pile of tears because I knew He would do just that. He specializes in showing His children the way.

I spent many days decreeing God's Word out loud. Things began to change in a slow progression to wellness. Over time, my symptoms left. I have been free of all Lyme symptoms for two years. This is a miracle. This journey has shaped my faith. Thank You, Lord for showing me the way!

Reflections

DAY

20

I Will See a Victory!

"In the course of time, David defeated the Philistines and subdued them, and he took Gath and its surrounding villages from the control of the Philistines. David also defeated the Moabites, and they became subject to him and brought him tribute.

"Moreover, David defeated Hadadezer king of Zobah, in the vicinity of Hamath, when he went to set up his monument at the Euphrates River. David captured a thousand of his chariots, seven thousand charioteers and twenty thousand foot soldiers. He hamstrung all but a hundred of the chariot horses.

"When the Arameans of Damascus came to help Hadadezer king of Zobah, David struck down twenty-two thousand of them. He put garrisons in the Aramean kingdom of Damascus, and the Arameans became subject to him and brought him tribute. The Lord gave David victory wherever he went.

"He put garrisons in Edom, and all the Edomites became subject to David. The Lord gave David victory wherever he went."
-1 Chronicles 18:1-6, 13

If you read about David's victories in 1 Chronicles 18, it's quite amazing. David had incredible leadership around him that multiplied his leadership anointing and strategy.[18] Who we surround ourselves with is key.

The Lord has taken me to 1 Chronicles 17 and 18 several times. There is something significant here for us, a new word as we enter this new season.

Everywhere David went, he had the victory of the Lord. And it doesn't seem like he just raised a toast to celebrate, he also took the plunder from the enemy. Every last item was his for the taking.

David had an intimate encounter with the Lord in 1 Chronicles 17. He longed to build a temple for the Lord since the Ark of the Covenant had only been in a tent. Instead, the Lord declared to David that He was going to build David a house and then promised him the rule and reign of his generations. The leadership anointing on David's life would be passed to his children. Even Jesus would come through the lineage of David. What an incredible declaration of promise.

David heard the promises of God and set out with vigor, conquest, and courage. The enemies of God and His people were about to fall. In fact, they wouldn't just fall, they would be plundered. David took their plunder and dedicated these things to the Lord to be used for the building of the temple that his son, Solomon, would construct at a later time.

"Your ceiling is your children's floor."
-Bill Johnson

I love this quote. Where you go with the Lord will be the places your children leap from in their callings. What you "store up" like Mary will be for your children to ponder and draw from.

David's heart for God was passed to Solomon and enabled him to build the temple to completion. The very plunder of the enemy's camps constructed a place of worship. How ironic.

> "Every victory and every enemy subdued was a testimony to the Lord's preserving power in the life and reign of David." -David Guzik

Jesus did this very thing at the cross, and He will manifest this very spiritual reality in your life. Don't think for a minute that the pain and places of warfare will be wasted. Your heart of worship is being constructed with the very hands of God, and He declares His victory and abundance over that.

"May God give you every desire of your heart
and carry out your every plan as you go to battle.
When you succeed, we will celebrate and shout for joy.
Flags will fly when victory is yours!
Yes, God will answer your prayers and we will praise him!
I know God gives me all that I ask for
and brings victory to his anointed king.
My deliverance cry will be heard in his holy heaven.
By his mighty hand miracles will manifest
through his saving strength."
-Psalm 20:4-6, TPT

This is my prayer for you today:

> Lord, I pray for Your manifest victory over Your daughter! May she walk in the victory You paid

for through Your very life, Jesus. You declare Your victory, Your freedom, Your deliverance, and Your healing over her today. And like David, I pray that You allow her to plunder the camps of the enemy and take back everything that has been taken from her - innocence, hope, provision, relationships, and love. Return it to her one-hundred-fold, in Jesus name. Hero of heaven, take her into spacious places of delight where You seat her at a feasting table and declare restoration and fullness and abundance.

The enemy will not have the last word over her past, present, or future. That is reserved for Your Word only. And the past season(s) will be for Your full redemption and justice. I pray for strength for her to believe Your goodness will rain down on her. Create in her a heart of worship as she waits and watches and believes for victory.

Lord, I command a blessing on the head of Your daughter and her generations, that her *"YES"* to this time of encounter and consecration results in victories in her life and the lives of her generations like she has never seen. May she fix her eyes on You, her great Victor and Champion!

Listen to this worship song via YouTube: "See a Victory" by Elevation Worship

Listen to this worship song via YouTube: "You are My Champion" by Bethel Music (featuring Dante Bowe)

Kristi's Story

In my walk with God, I have found there is a space in time where I sometimes feel stuck. It's the space between asking the Lord for a miracle and the waiting for Him to show up. That space can feel barren, leave us questioning, and, if we let it, open a host of lies from the evil one to flood our minds. What do we do when we find ourselves in that space in between the "ask" and the miracle?

When I was 16, I was diagnosed with an untreatable, irreversible kidney disease that should have taken my life. But God intervened and supernaturally healed me completely. I experienced Jehovah-Rapha, the God who heals, and am forever grateful for that answered prayer. But I've also experienced His silence on other desires of my heart. I asked the Lord for a specific breakthrough eight years ago and have yet to see that prayer answered in the way I would like. I tell you this because I know you can relate, the answered prayer versus the "perceived" unanswered prayer.

Keep asking. Oh, if we could have eyes to see the heavenly realm and know what is being fought on our behalf. This is the opportunity for you to lean into what you know to be true about God. Dig into Scripture and write down everything you see that describes the character of who God is, fix your eyes on the one who created you, intentionally shut out the lies of the enemy and hold tight to the promises of God. Whether He answers your prayer the way you desire or in the timing you wish for is where you can get stuck. Focus instead on the fact that He is working. Rest in that truth.

And take heart; that place of waiting is where we grow deep spiritual roots. It is an act of worship to trust God in the midst of the unseen.

Those roots we grow by the streams of uncertainty are what carry us through life's future trials. I pray that in your "space in between," you find unexplainable peace, supernatural joy, hopeful anticipation, and a season of spiritual flourishing as you fix your eyes on Him.

Reflections

DAY 21

It Will Cost Something

"Then the angel of the Lord ordered Gad to tell David to go up and build an altar to the Lord on the threshing floor of Araunah the Jebusite. So David went up in obedience to the word that Gad had spoken in the name of the Lord.

"While Araunah was threshing wheat, he turned and saw the angel; his four sons who were with him hid themselves. Then David approached, and when Araunah looked and saw him, he left the threshing floor and bowed down before David with his face to the ground.

"David said to him, 'Let me have the site of your threshing floor so I can build an altar to the Lord, that the plague on the people may be stopped. Sell it to me at the full price.'

"Araunah said to David, 'Take it! Let my lord the king do whatever pleases him. Look, I will give the oxen for the burnt offerings, the threshing sledges for the wood, and the wheat for the grain offering. I will give all this.'

"But King David replied to Araunah, 'No, I insist on paying the full price. I will not take for the Lord what is yours or sacrifice a burnt offering that costs me nothing.'

"So David paid Araunah six hundred shekels of gold for the site. David built an altar to the Lord there and sacrificed burnt offerings and fellowship offerings. He called on the Lord, and the Lord answered him with fire from heaven on the altar of burnt offering."
-1 Chronicles 21:18-26

We read yesterday of the victories the Lord gave to David on every side. The Lord gave David victories everywhere he went. The story turns a bit after a significant period of time, and we see David fall into submission to the schemes of Satan. Huge bummer. But David is not left in his prideful predicament.

The Lord invites David to meet Him on the threshing floor in worship. According to commentaries, this threshing floor of Ornan was on Mount Moriah, the same hill where Abraham went to sacrifice Isaac, and just across the hilltops where our Jesus died on the cross.

David asked to buy this threshing floor at its full price. David would not sacrifice to the Lord that which cost him nothing. The very place where the chaff was separated from the wheat would be a place of worship and sacrifice. This same place eventually became the location of Solomon's temple.

> "David knew that it would not be a gift nor a sacrifice unto the Lord if it did not cost him something. He didn't look for the cheapest way possible to please God." -David Guzik

> "Where there is true, strong love to Jesus, it will cost us something. Love is the costliest of all undertakings … But what shall we mind if we gain Christ? You cannot give up for Him without regaining everything you have renounced, but purified and transfigured." -F.B. Meyer

Sister, we will count the cost. Every day we will consider the cost of our pursuit of Jesus. We will either linger with Him for a while and wrap our life around His life, or we will go on with life as normal. There will be a sacrifice to going deeper.

Yes, we will miss the things that used to consume our time and our heart. But He will come with fire and consume the sacrifices for all to see the glory of the One we love and adore. My heart's cry is for an army of worshiping women to arise in this hour who are so consumed by their love for their Bridegroom. What seems like a sacrifice will be a laid down life of worship.

He is worth it. I will declare this for all my days. He is worth every seeming "sacrifice" we make.

John Maisel, the Founder of East-West Ministries International, calls this sacrifice of the worship of my life, "the martyrdom of my heart for Jesus sake." Jesus is coming for His precious Bride, who is dressed in righteousness, purity, holiness, and single-minded pursuit of Him.

I encourage you to have a very honest conversation with the Lord about what this "cost" looks like between the two of you. He will answer the desires of your heart.

We are going to begin a journey into our calling and commissioning by the Spirit of God. Buckle up; it's about to get even better. Listen to the song from Day 1 of our encounter and get ready!

Listen to this worship song via YouTube: "King of Kings" by Hillsong Worship

Jen's Story

My daughter, adopted at age 4, is my commissioning by the Spirit. Raising her, especially after my husband passed away, is the greatest sacrifice of my life. The time, tears, and suffering at the hands of this child, for this child, have all been for Jesus.

I wanted and begged to quit - give up - many, many times. God won't let me. I am so thankful He won't let me, but I get angry that He won't let me.

My relationship with my other children has been strained since the day we brought her home. My eldest has more trauma from his adopted sister than from the death of his earthly father. My relationship with my new husband suffers as I care for my daughter.

But, because God is so good, He created my new husband exactly to care for me as I care for her. My life is a sacrifice for the life of my daughter. I am judged for it all the time. By family and friends alike. Satan tries all the time to break me.

But God designed me specifically for this job. I will never quit. Even when I want to. Even when I beg to. He sustains me. He carries me. He loves me. He wipes my tears. He holds my hand. He draws me in. He shows me the way. He lets me yell at Him. He washes me clean. He understands my pain. He continues to ask. And I continue to respond, *"YES."*

Reflections

DAY

22

His Resurrection ... Your Commissioning

We are moving into a forward focus of vision as we enter the final lap of this season of consecration together. I think it's quite appropriate to begin with the story of Mary, the first person commissioned by Jesus after His resurrection.

"Now Mary stood outside the tomb crying. As she wept, she bent over to look into the tomb and saw two angels in white, seated where Jesus' body had been, one at the head and the other at the foot. They asked her, 'Woman, why are you crying?' 'They have taken my Lord away,' she said, 'and I don't know where they have put him.' At this, she turned around and saw Jesus standing there, but she did not realize that it was Jesus. He asked her, 'Woman, why are you crying? Who is it you are looking for?' Thinking he was the gardener, she said, 'Sir, if you have carried him away, tell me where you have put him, and I will get him.' Jesus said to her, 'Mary.' She turned toward him and cried out in Aramaic, 'Rabboni!' (which means 'Teacher'). Jesus said, 'Do not hold on to me, for I have not yet ascended to the Father. Go instead to my brothers and

tell them, I am ascending to my Father and your Father, to my God and your God.' Mary Magdalene went to the disciples with the news: 'I have seen the Lord!' And she told them that he had said these things to her."
-John 20:11-18

I think this is one of the sweetest moments between Jesus and His dear friend, Mary. I am tearful as I write this. There was no one Mary wanted more in that moment than Jesus. She wept because none of this made sense. She wasn't confident in His resurrection. All she knew was He was dead and now He was missing. He was the One her heart longed for and wondered about.

But true to His character, Jesus wasn't far away. He came right to Mary and called her by name.

"Her eyes fail her, but her ears could not mistake that voice saying her name. Many had called her by that name. She had been wont to hear it many times a day from many lips; but only One had spoken it with that intonation."
-F.B. Meyer

Just as Jesus, the greatest liberator of women, would have it, Mary became the first witness of the resurrection of Christ. A woman was the first person He commissioned to go and tell.

His heart for women to arise and "go" into the world and "tell" what we have seen and heard is trumpeting from the throne room of heaven in this hour!

Daughters of the Most High God, this is your hour of commissioning.

We have stood and wept at our places of doubt, despair, discouragement, disillusionment, and defeat for long enough. I know seasons of hardship; I shared some of my own. But it's in that garden of the empty tomb where Jesus meets us. It is here, at the empty tomb, where all those realities are given a new name of hope, faith, vision, joy, clarity, and victory. We can look at the empty grave and know there's a better word spoken over our lives. The grave is empty, and Jesus calls us by name as He looks with eyes of compassion and love. That very compassion becomes the compelling force to which He sends us out.

Mary ran from that garden place to the disciples because she had a new revelation, a new testimony, and a new day to declare. Jesus conquered the grave. Whether they believed or not was not up to her. She just went when Jesus said, "Go!"

I encourage you to turn your gaze from a place of bewilderment to see the face of Jesus and His look of compassion and love. There was a destiny written over your life before the foundations of the world. It is not for doubt and mediocrity, but for passion and compassion. There's a dying world waiting for you to turn and run from the empty tomb to those who are waiting to hear!

He has something else for you and it's coming. There's a resounding "go" in His heart and on His lips for you.

> Lord, make this passage come alive to my sister. You are calling Your daughter to move out in her authority and commissioning.
>
> Meet her in the places where she needs to see Your resurrection power and let her declare with conviction the transforming love and presence of her Jesus. Fill

her with faith to step into all that You have set before her. Make her a bold and courageous daughter of the King.

Listen to this Worship song via YouTube: "Still" by Amanda Cook

Mindi's Story

This month of pausing each day to hear the Lord speak through this devotion has been just what I needed. I've been in a time of transition. Transition is exciting for some, but in my case, it's been a time of grieving. I wasn't seeing what God was preparing me to step into. I liked the old way of doing things. So, I didn't move. He was calling me to step out on my own, away from a team in ministry I was comfortable with. I didn't think my time was up, but things shifted, and God said, "It's time to move into the promised land I have for you and your calling."

I am a prophetic painter.[19] I've spent the last two years working on a huge project, painting each book of the Bible. It was a season of complete focus in the secret place with the Lord, seeing Him and getting to know Him in Scripture through art.

As the season ended, I had plans of what would happen next, but things shifted differently than I thought. I grieved in private the things not going the way I anticipated. The Lord began to speak to my heart, "It's time to take your story and testimony into a new arena, into teaching and sharing My testimony of the journey you had painting with Me." I didn't want to leave the old season. But deep down I knew the Lord had a new thing - a stretching into speaking, which is outside my comfort zone. (I'm used to having my back to a crowd or painting by myself in my studio.) He wants to transition me out of the old and into the new.

When I read this day's entry, it resonated with me. Mary was crying over the death of Jesus, grieving her time with Him in person. But He was about to do something new, to commission her to go. He needed to die in order to fulfill the Father's plans. It was for our benefit He left this way. None of it made sense to Mary at the time. But she recognized His voice calling her by name.

It is much the same with me. I must lay down the old, accept what has happened, and obey the voice of the Lord into where He is leading. I must trust that He knows the best for me. Now go!

I can see God has bigger plans for us than we can see in each phase of our life. I want to be a woman that arises to her calling, testifying of His love and story written through me. When I read, "Daughters of the Most High God, this is your hour of commissioning," I felt a clarity and courage to release the old and step fully into the new. Mary had a new day to declare, and so do I.

Lord, today I lay down my plans and trust fully in Your plans through my life and through my art. Lord, teach me to see from Your perspective, even when things don't make sense. Fill me with faith to step out into the unknown. "There is a dying world waiting for You to turn and run from the empty tomb to those who are waiting to hear!"

The crazy confirming thing about what Julie wrote in today's devotion is something the Lord told me at the beginning of my art journey through the Bible. He said, "There is a dying world who needs to see the beauty of the Word through art."

Reflections

DAY

23

Awaken and Arise

"'Come, follow me,' Jesus said, 'and I will send you out to fish for people.' At once they left their nets and followed him.

"Going on from there, he saw two other brothers, James son of Zebedee and his brother John. They were in a boat with their father Zebedee, preparing their nets. Jesus called them, and immediately they left the boat and their father and followed him."

-Matthew 4:19-22

If I could translate Jesus' invitation to these guys, I bet He was saying, "Hey guys, it's time to start your impossible."

As I picture the guys sitting in their boats, doing the usual as expert fisherman, I doubt they were dreaming of changing the world. Their simple and routine lives were immediately changed at the very invitation of Jesus to "come." Jesus' invitation was wrapped in the heart of, "I will change the world through you." But they had no idea what was ahead of them. They just made an immediate decision to leave it all and follow Him, which ultimately cost them everything.

Following Jesus was and is worth it all.

I remember on the first women's "Extreme Trip" to South Asia, I walked up to a couple who had built a little store on stilts at their village entrance. It was put together with some wood and tin. They sold a few different flavors of potato chips, water, candies, and gum. During the course of telling them about the love of Jesus, I asked them, "What are the dreams you have in your heart for your life?"

They looked at me and looked at each other, laughed out loud, and said, "We can't dream." They believed their only option was survival without the possibility to dream for anything better. What chance do dreams have in survival mode? They weren't expecting anything different than the routine, day-to-day need to make it to tomorrow.

I can't imagine what it's like to not be able to dream about God doing impossible things through my life. You and I were created to partner with God so entire nations could hear the gospel message. Over 3 billion people have yet to hear the name of Jesus. We were created to do even greater things than Jesus did, as impossible as that sounds. [20]

Before the foundations of the world, God wrote a grand story of your life on adventure with Him. There's a destiny He has authored, and a dying world is waiting for you to "get out of the boat" at His invitation, grip His hand, and go.

"Water is waiting to be walked on again."
-Bill Johnson

We were created to invade the impossible. Impossibility is what Jesus longs to bring forth through your very life.

At the age of 12, my parents sold our house in California, quit their jobs, and followed Jesus to Germany. It made no rational sense, but they knew God was calling them. Some of our extended family members were in a perpetual state of disbelief at this preposterous idea.

Their faith resulted in something I could have never dreamed of - today my daughters have a passion for the nations. God deposited, in my parent's sheer *"YES"* of faith, a calling in our bloodline for the nations and for the gospel. And it is bearing fruit in my daughters.

Lizzy, my oldest daughter, and I went on a mission trip to South Asia a while back. During that trip, I heard her pray for healing over a witch doctor and share the gospel with person after person who didn't know the goodness of God.

This is the same "living" that Jesus wanted for His guys when He called them that day. It's the same "living" the Holy Spirit is inviting us to step into with passion, fervency, and urgency.

God has placed a grand invitation before us and has sealed it with His blood and His promises. He's inviting us to pursue Jesus with passion and to be the ones who change history. We were created to be game changers. Somehow the American dream has kept us tied to building a life that culture says we must pursue. We stand at a precipice of a grand "crossover" into the promises He has destined for us.

Do we pursue Jesus with reckless abandon, or do we run to what is comfortable and familiar?

What if my parents had said, "No, we aren't going to follow You. It's too far outside of our comfort zone. We've never been there before. What about retirement? What about the new pool we just put in? What about the kids who are in their formative years?" They would have given up the grandest adventure with Jesus. My daughters and I may not have the love for nations that we do. Their *"YES!"* literally impacted nations and generations.

It's time to start your impossible! A dying world is waiting for an encounter with the God of the universe through your very life.

> Jesus, I pray that You would call me out of my boat of comfort and familiarity and take me on the grandest adventures with You that my mind can't even dream! Release faith and courage to say *"YES"* when I hear Your voice.

Listen to this Worship song via YouTube: "Into Faith I Go" by Pat Barrett

Allison's Story

There have been times when I have known God was whispering to my heart, stirring my soul, inviting me to adventure with Him, especially in relation to Romans 15:20-21. When I first heard this passage in college, my spirit said, *"YES! YES! YES!"* I didn't know who, when, where, or how, but I put a stake in the ground and said if I could be anything, this was it.

Now years later, I am watching Him unfold this calling on my life. I am reminded that the resources for the impossible are in Him. The impossible of hearing a man's testimony in a remote village on the other side of the world who was healed, in Jesus' name, of debilitating pain in his legs.

The impossible in the Middle East to see a man laying lifeless on the street a few feet in front of a stopped bus. As men carried his limp body to the sidewalk, my friend and I prayed at the Holy Spirit's prompting for this man to sit up, and have life breathed into his body. As the words were spoken aloud, the Lord did the impossible.

The impossible of being the messenger of good news to over 70 people in five days in South Asia, sharing with unreached people who have never heard of Jesus. A government school's administrator invited me to share the gospel, and on that day, the entire school, including administrators, all prayed with me.

By responding *"YES!"* I see and live the adventure and the impossible of the gospel. I can't help but wonder if maybe you also sense a stirring and hear His voice calling, "Come and follow me." My friends, He does not disappoint. Say *"YES!"*

Reflections

DAY

24

HE WILL BE TENDER WITH YOU

"Aware of this, Jesus withdrew from that place. A large crowd followed him, and he healed all who were ill. He warned them not to tell others about him. This was to fulfill what was spoken through the prophet Isaiah:

'Here is my servant whom I have chosen,
the one I love, in whom I delight;
I will put my Spirit on him,
and he will proclaim justice to the nations.
He will not quarrel or cry out;
no one will hear his voice in the streets.
A bruised reed he will not break,
and a smoldering wick he will not snuff out,
till he has brought justice through to victory.
In his name the nations will put their hope.'"
-Matthew 12:15-21

God gave me a dream as I was writing about His commissioning words. In my dream, I sat with a couple pregnant with twins. She was a friend in my dream, but I don't know her in real life. She shared with me that her babies were not growing as they should. She was helpless to do anything. This Scripture came out of my mouth to her:

"A bruised reed he will not break, and a smoldering wick he will not snuff out."
-Matthew 12:20a

In another scene, I was in a board room full of people and John Maisel, the Founder of East-West, walked in. He has pulmonary fibrosis in real life. He still had this disease in my dream but was on fire for Jesus while his body fought for life. And again, this Scripture came out of my mouth:

"A bruised reed he will not break, and a smoldering wick he will not snuff out."
-Matthew 12:20a

I decided to study this portion of Scripture because I think it's a divine interruption for us at this juncture. The Lord can and will commission you to your destiny, but He wants you to know that He is gentle and tender and loving toward you and all you have endured. In fact, the places you have overcome are going to be your places of greatest authority in ministry.

I love the compassion of Jesus to heal everyone He was with that day. It was uncommon that He healed every single person in the places He ministered, but He did that day.

We see this anointed, chosen, loved Son of God who still serves us every day and lives to intercede for us. His ministry to us has not stopped. He will not break a bruised read or snuff out a smoldering wick.

> "This is another reference to the gentle character of Jesus. A reed is a fairly fragile plant, yet if a reed is bruised the Servant will handle it so gently that He will not break it. And if falx, used as a wick for an oil lamp, does not flame but only smokes, He will not quench it into extinguishing. Instead, the Servant will gently nourish the smoking flax, fanning it into flame again." -David Guzik

I believe the Lord wants us to know that all our failures, hang-ups, mistakes, and weaknesses are dealt with by a loving God. He is tender toward us and cares intimately for each of us.

> "Jesus sees the value in a bruised reed, even when no one else can. He can make beautiful music come from a bruised reed, as He puts His strength in it. Though a smoking flax is good for nothing, Jesus knows it is valuable for what it can be when it is refreshed with oil. Many of us are like the bruised reed, and we need to be strengthened with might through His Spirit in the inner man (Ephesians 3:16). Others are like the smoking flax and can only burn brightly for the Lord again when we are drenched in oil, with a constant supply coming, as we are filled with the Holy Spirit." -David Guzik

The Lord is familiar with your frailty, but He is also convinced of the power and authority and purposes of Christ living and residing in you. He's so convinced of this that He will stop at nothing to pursue your heart and get you ready for what is ahead. You are not disqualified by brokenness. You are being positioned in even greater authority for what is ahead.

The very places He has given you victory will be what you bring to other people who are in desperate need of freedom, hope, and healing. He is making you a warrior in the secret place. The Lord placed this word on my heart for you:

> I Am indeed opening the floodgates on My daughter. I Am bringing her to sit at My feet. I want to tell her things, but I also want to build this love relationship and friendship with her. I Am going to let her behold My goodness. It will be an awakening in her life that will transfer her gaze on Me. I Am going to set her free of the things that anchor her and hold her back.
>
> You will watch and be amazed at My goodness as I lavish My love on My daughters. I have told you over and over that these are the days of joyous expectation and wonder. We are approaching a transition point in history. Those who have a heart for Me will have their fires flamed. There is a line in the sand for those who will live boldly in this next era. New wine and new oil for those who are ready to receive!

Listen to this worship song via YouTube: "He Made Me, He Loves Me" by Ben and Noelle Kilgore

Taylor's Story

Two years ago, while listening to a Charles Spurgeon sermon, God's presence fell on me like never before. This was after a three-month wilderness period where I thought I'd committed the unpardonable sin because of God's silence. This was also the time I came to truly know Jesus as my Lord and personal Savior.

Being in the wilderness was the worst and best time of my life. I was so encouraged by Spurgeon's ministering on the part of God's word from Isaiah 42:3, KJV, that reads, *"a bruised reed He will not break and the smoking flax he will not quench."* Spurgeon's interpretation was focused on what little bit of good is in us has been placed there through His Spirit. So even though it may be a little bit of faithfulness, God is not going to destroy it or us because what is in us and what He plans to use was orchestrated by Him.

In this devotional, Julie shares how Isaiah 42 was fulfilled by Jesus, and she addresses the gentleness of the Lord from a different angle. She teaches, "The Lord can and will commission you to your destiny, but He wants you to know that He is gentle and tender and loving toward you and all you have endured. In fact, the places you have overcome are going to be your places of greatest authority in ministry."

The first time I heard this scripture, I was burdened the months prior to hearing it. But now, at this stage of my spiritual growth, these encouraging and impactful words have propelled me even further in my faith and belief of what God wants to do through my life. He wants to use what He placed inside me. What a sweet reminder of God's gentleness toward His children.

Reflections

DAY

25

ARISE, OUR LYDIAS

"From Troas we sailed a straight course to the island of Samothrace, and the next day to Neapolis. Finally we reached Philippi, a major city in the Roman colony of Macedonia, and we remained there for a number of days.

"When the Sabbath day came, we went outside the gates of the city to the nearby river, for there appeared to be a house of prayer and worship there. Sitting on the riverbank we struck up a conversation with some of the women who had gathered there.

"One of them was Lydia, a businesswoman from the city of Thyatira who was a dealer of exquisite purple cloth and a Jewish convert. While Paul shared the good news with her, God opened her heart to receive Paul's message. She devoted herself to the Lord, and we baptized her and her entire family. Afterward she urged us to stay in her home, saying, 'Since I am now a believer in the Lord, come and stay in my house.' So we were persuaded to stay there.

"So Paul and Silas left the prison and went back to Lydia's house, where they met with the believers and comforted and encouraged them before departing."
-Acts 16:11-15, 40, TPT

Paul was led to Europe by the Holy Spirit where he met Lydia. Not only was she the first convert on the continent of Europe, but she was also a successful businesswoman who dealt with valuable and luxurious products.

Due to the expenses involved in her profession, she most likely not only interacted with the elite of her day, but she acquired wealth in her occupation. Her home was most likely large with servants to assist her. In fact, she showed great hospitality to Paul and Silas and the other believers. This is evidence of the openness and generosity of Lydia's life. She became the founder of the Church at Philippi after her conversion.

Philippians is a beautiful love letter from Paul addressed to a healthy and growing church. Lydia was a successful businesswoman in a prosperous city who was likely mentored by Paul and equipped by the Holy Spirit to birth a new church and help the believers grow.

> "Lydia not only sold her dyes—she served her Saviour. She stayed in business that she might have the money to help God's servants in their ministry. How her generous care of Paul and Silas, and of many others, must have cheered their hearts. Lydia was, first of all, a consecrated Christian, then a conscientious businesswoman who continued to sell her purple dyes for the glory of God. When we reach heaven, we shall find this 'seller of purple' wearing more superior garments, robes not stained even with the notable dye of Thyatira, but washed and made white in the blood of the Lamb."[21]

Both Jesus and Paul had no problem teaching, calling, empowering, and equipping women to minister in their giftedness and abilities.

Jewish culture did everything to sideline and silence women. Jesus came as the great liberator and Paul followed right in step.

> "Sadly, many believers have very little idea about the real nature of the Christ they are following. For the most part, the Church has domesticated the Lion of the tribe of Judah, relegating Him to a household pet or imprisoning Him behind barads of some religious zoo. But the truth is that when Jesus walked the earth, He was a counterculture radical who not only healed the sick and raised the dead, but also liberated the oppressed and set the captives free. Women were at the top of His list!" -Kris Vallotton[22]

As I sought the Lord for revelation on these last remaining days of devotions, the Holy Spirit reminded me of Lydia. Since we are in our commissioning portion of this encounter, I want to both validate and encourage our businesswomen who are building the Kingdom of God through your brilliance, giftedness, faithfulness, excellence, and surrender.

I think there's an idea that has permeated Christendom that only those "in ministry" are serving the Lord. In reality, it takes the whole Bride of Christ who are empowered by the Holy Spirit and assigned to their place of calling to build and expand the Kingdom. Oh, that we would move in unity and momentum together.

Our calling is to arise in this hour and carry forth the gospel with passion and urgency into every fabric of society where God has placed us. I believe our business leaders have a unique role in this hour.

To the Lydias reading this, I honor your giftedness and assignments in business and declare increase to everything your hands touch.

I pray wisdom and revelation to build and expand the dreams God has placed inside of you for new business ventures. I pray for people to come alongside you to help fund these ventures and connect you with others who will multiply what God has put on your heart. I pray for an increase of clients, customers, referrals, and marketing teams. I pray that as God brings you increase, you will turn it to build His church all over the world, just as Lydia did.

Lydia didn't stop with what God had given her hands to do business-wise. The first church born through her life, giftedness, and teachable spirit impacted an entire continent. God is assigning nations to us, and this may be the role you play to see the church expand across a global landscape. Let it be so, in Jesus' name!

Listen to this worship song via YouTube: "Spirit Lead Me" by Michael Ketterer and Influence Music

Heather's Story

I've never wanted to be a Lydia. I wanted to either inspire multitudes from a stage or live in an African hut as a career missionary. Or both. But (in my dramatic opinion), the absolute worst imaginable service of my life would be to work in sales. I believed the lie that being a salesperson meant, "I wasn't good enough for full-time ministry."

On Day 25 of this journey, I was at an all-day training for hearing aid dispensers, feeling discouraged. Because I was fasting, I couldn't enjoy the delicious catered lunch, so I sipped my broth alone and read my email devotional.

When I got to the part about Lydia selling expensive items, using her large home to host, and how she wasn't called to leave her business but to serve the Lord with her resources, I started weeping. It's like I'd never even considered Lydia before.

I was so shaken that I walked through the large conference center to process my thoughts and ask the Holy Spirit for more. As I walked, I acknowledged that I *do* pray boldly for healing in the name of Jesus for almost every person who walks into my office. I also realized that I've been able to sow into many more ministries than before. We use our large home for God's glory and desire to host missionaries who need housing on furlough. As I thought through these things, I ended up in a lobby and sat down to journal.

Just then I recognized where I was. I'd only been in this place once, seven years earlier, and I had a clear flashback. That day in this same lobby, I'd successfully negotiated a business deal on behalf of a nonprofit organization. Before that day, I'd never realized that I possessed this type of hidden skill. Now, seven years later, I was teary and in awe that the Holy Spirit had led me back to the memory. It was like He was whispering, "I know what I'm doing with you, Heather. You have an important place in my kingdom. Don't despise this season. I've gifted you in sales for a purpose."

I really wanted Him to promise that eventually He would send me to the "front lines," but I trust Him and I'm embracing being a Lydia ... at least for now.

Reflections

DAY

26

LET YOUR FAITH TESTIFY

"If I'm not doing the beautiful works that my Father sent me to do, then don't believe me. But if you see me doing the beautiful works of God upon the earth, then you should at least believe the evidence of the miracles, even if you don't believe my words! Then you would come to experience me and be convinced that I am in the Father and the Father is in me."
-John 10:37-38, TPT

"So he replied to the messengers, 'Go back and report to John what you have seen and heard: The blind receive sight, the lame walk, those who have leprosy are cleansed, the deaf hear, the dead are raised, and the good news is proclaimed to the poor.'"
-Luke 7:22

"He replied, 'Because your faith is much too small. What I'm about to tell you is true. If you have faith as small as a mustard seed, it is enough. You can say to this mountain, Move from here to there. And it will move. Nothing will be impossible for you.'"
-Matthew 17:20, NIRV

"That night our Lord appeared to Paul and stood before him and said, 'Receive miracle power. For just as you have spoken for me in Jerusalem, you will also speak for me in Rome.'"
-Acts 23:11, TPT

Jesus testified about the Father to an unbelieving nation through miracles, signs, and wonders. He said, "Even if you don't believe me, believe the miracles." The Jewish people wanted a sign before they would believe. Yet, His whole life testified to the Father and His Kingdom.

Paul is given the calling to take the gospel to the Gentiles after his encounter with Jesus on the road to Damascus. He traversed every place, nation, and city where God told him to go. His feet were not still unless he was in prison.

And then his heart traversed and scribed the letters that became part of God's love letter to His people. Paul could not help but testify about Jesus to the rulers, religious, and spiritually hungry. He couldn't keep silent because Christ was his very life.

Paul had to testify because nations and entire people groups had yet to know Jesus. He couldn't be silent and hope people would be set free in those places. He couldn't wait for someone else to go into the next city or country. God asked him to go.

Thirty-two years of ministry is all Paul had.[23] He planted, built up, fortified, strengthened, encouraged, charged, and expanded the church. Today his letters and his life of surrender continue to speak to us.

God's Word never ceases to be relevant. His miracles never stop pointing us to Himself. It's all about testifying to every last part of who we are!

Now it's your turn. The baton has been passed to you. This is your time, your commissioning, your hour to impact history. Consider answering these questions in your journal as you bring them before the Lord:

- Does my life point to Jesus?
- Does His word come forth from my life?
- Do I build up, strengthen, and encourage my brothers and sisters?
- Does my life give space and faith for the miraculous?
- Does my life testify to the goodness and power of Jesus?
- Could I explain Him in a court of accusers?
- Is there any evidence to convict me of living in impossibility?
- Do I speak to mountains and tell them to move?
- Is everything in my life possible for me?
- Do I step my feet into impossible moments waiting for Jesus to show up? Or, do I sit and analyze it in unbelief, fear, and intimidation?
- Do I believe Him enough to make Him known? Or do I wait for Him to move first to validate me?
- What if I stepped out, took a chance, and let Him show up in the way Jesus did when He walked the earth?

Stop and pray:

> Lord, ignite my faith for impossibility. Teach me how to pray for people and situations without hesitation. Raise me up to lead the charge into courage. May my life testify and give evidence to the power and presence

> of Jesus. Lord, I ask that I not be a motorboat tied to the dock of unbelief, mediocrity, possibility, and fear of looking foolish. Cut those ropes free. I pray that I would surf on the waves of the power and authority of "Christ in me, the hope of glory."

Until the gospel is preached to the whole world, this is our mandate:

> Lord, I pray that You would use our lives to testify to the miraculous, to truth, to His goodness, and to His Presence. Let the Church arise in this hour with a courageous declaration that we will not be quiet any longer. Jesus, You died so we would be the most courageous people on the face of the earth. Then You came to live inside of us to secure that reality. Lord, would You mobilize the women in this next decade to be a force for the Kingdom of Heaven. Will You download vision and clear, clear strategy for each one of us, so we won't wonder any longer about what You have for us. May we know it with passion and conviction and joy. In the marvelous name of Jesus.

Listen to this worship song via YouTube: "So Will I (100 Billion X)" Lyric Video - Hillsong United

Jessica's Story

Living in a southern suburb of Dallas with our three young daughters and teaching at public schools, my husband and I were exhausted, feeling the pace of life and work were suffocating us. Our hearts desire is to invest in eternal matters, to build God's Kingdom rather than our own. I joined this 31-day fast with the anticipation of receiving direction from God. He did just that. He directed me to leave my teaching job and minister to my family by being a stay-at-home mom. I talked with my husband, who was on board. The day after I left my teaching job, my husband received a call from a previous employer, offering him a position with higher pay, more paid time off, and flexible hours. The Lord immediately provided the confirmation to our decision through financial increase and more time at home for my husband.

I have always wanted to build the kingdom of God and teach our children to love the Lord with all their heart, mind, soul, and strength. My husband is from Brazil; he attended an American missionary school while growing up in Brazil. Around the time I gave my two weeks' notice for my job, my husband received a call about available positions at the school he attended as a child. We had not talked about moving to Brazil, but it was always something we were willing to do if it was God's plan. We spent time praying for God's direction, and at His prompting, we leaned into this possibility. My husband sent an email to the superintendent, and his response to us was overwhelmingly positive.

Through a lot of prayer and seeking and listening to the Lord, we accepted the position at the school and will be moving to Brazil this summer. There is so much to do before we go, but sometimes following the Lord is like living in a whirlwind. I trust He is guiding our every move.

One of the catapults that moved us to this point was the time spent fasting with the Arise women and devotionals. There is fruit! He is sending us out.

Reflections

DAY 27

SHE'S GETTING READY!

"As for me, because I am innocent, I will see your face until I see you for who you really are. Then I will awaken with your form and be fully satisfied, fulfilled in the revelation of your glory in me!"
-Psalm 17:15, TPT

"Then I heard something like the shout of a vast multitude, and like the boom of many pounding waves, and like the roar of mighty peals of thunder, saying, 'Hallelujah! For the Lord our God, the Almighty, [the Omnipotent, the Ruler of all] reigns. Let us rejoice and shout for joy! Let us give Him glory and honor, for the marriage of the Lamb has come [at last] and His bride (the redeemed) has prepared herself.'"
-Revelation 19:7, AMP

Before writing Day 27, I awoke to the words, "I have never known a love like this." I spent an hour trying to find the song and came across the worship moment I posted below. Close your eyes and enter the song, picturing Jesus' look of love and adoration for you, His spotless Bride.

"Awakening" is defined as an act of waking from sleep; an act or moment of becoming suddenly aware of something. I have been praying for you this month to draw nearer and nearer to the Lord. I have prayed you would endure until the end and glean everything you are tilling from your time with Jesus each day. I am praying for an awakening over the Bride of Christ in this glorious hour as the army of sons and daughters arises.

The Wedding Feast of the Lamb is the very culmination of history that erupts in worship and praise to the One who deserves it all. Jesus will be our great reward and the One and Only our heart adores. We will be His inheritance, presented to Him as spotless and ready. We await this day with eager anticipation.

But how do we prepare for this day? I asked the Lord about what it looks like to prepare for our Wedding Day to Jesus. Three things came to mind as I sat with Him.

First, "My people must walk in the 'It is finished' of the cross." Everything is paid for by His blood. Every sin is erased. Every chain is broken. Your freedom and healing are accomplished because of the cross. We don't add anything to our righteousness. We are righteous, blameless, holy, redeemed, set free, anointed, and awakened. This is the truest essence of grace. We add nothing to the cross because He declared, "It is finished!"

Second, "You are dressed in robes of righteousness, purity, and holiness." Your garments were given to you a great cost. It's not something you take off and put on. It's who you are. What you believe about yourself is how you will conduct your life. Do you believe you were set apart and marked for the glory of God? Our preparation for "that day" starts now. We are getting ready for the most magnificent wedding in all of history.

Last, "It's time to cease chasing the pleasures of the world and fix your gaze on Me." Our addiction to busyness keeps us entertained. But He has even more for us than earthly pleasures and worldly gain.

We don't want to be entertained into captivity.
We want to be captivated into wonder!

There is a song, your wedding song, that your Bridegroom is singing over you. It is to woo your heart that you would awaken and say, "I've never known a love like this!" I pray that you would hear His song and that your heart would beat with a new rhythm. It's the rhythm of heaven that joins the sound of the multitudes around the throne whose anthem gives Jesus the honor and glory and praise that He deserves.

There is nothing beating in my heart more for the Bride of Christ than a rally cry to run to her first love. He is moving heaven and earth for you to awaken to the reality of His never-ending love for you! It's your identity. It's what makes you who you are.

We want to be dressed and ready now for that day. But it takes asking Him to do it in us first. We respond to Him and make ourselves more and more available to Him taking up more and more residency in our lives. He will consume as much as we are willing to give to Him. He's a gentleman like that. I don't want to have just one shoe on with a veil as I run down the aisle to Him. I want to be dressed from head to toe, being made ready for that day, now!

Lord Jesus, consume every inch of my life. I declare Your beauty, Your worth, Your wonder, and Your glory. You are magnificent and deserving of the worship of my very life. Make me ready for the Wedding Feast of the Lamb. Lord, I ask You to cease useless activity and break the yoke of busyness. May my life be caught up, wrapped inside, and overflowing with a love for You that You deposit deep within me. May I be a single focused, radical lover of You, my Jesus!

Listen to this worship song via YouTube: "Jesus You're Beautiful (I'll Never Look Away)" by Peyton Allen

Yvonne's Story

My eating issues have been continual for many years. Often, I am reminded by the Word of God what my heart attitude should be in this matter. Throughout this 31-day journey, God used Scripture to teach me how to position myself before Him in worship.

"Therefore, I urge you, brothers and sisters, in view of God's mercy, to offer your bodies as a living sacrifice, holy and pleasing to God—this is your true and proper worship."
-Romans 12:1

Then, while I was praying, God gave me a vision of being a severely overweight person, so large I could not do anything except sit. I saw myself mindlessly consuming empty calories. Through that vision, I saw how my eating issues are the detestable opposite of my true and honoring worship to the Lord. This is the opposite of being holy and pleasing to Him. It is the opposite of offering my body as a living sacrifice.

My prayer for this new season is an echo from the first day of this devotional: Jesus, I invite You to take me to new heights and depths of revelation and intimacy. Take me there, and I will follow You. By faith, I say, "I'm ready!"

Reflections

DAY

28

It's Time to be "Reinstated"

"'Even if the mountains were to crumble
and the hills disappear,
my heart of steadfast, faithful love
will never leave you,
and my covenant of peace with you will never be shaken,'
says Yahweh,
whose love and compassion will never give up on you.
'You unhappy one, storm-tossed and troubled,
I am ready to rebuild you with precious stones,
and embed your foundation with sapphires.
I will make your towers of rubies,
your gates of sparkling jewels,
and all your walls of precious, delightful stones.'"
-Isaiah 54:10-12, TPT

"Yahweh will always guide you where to go and what to do.
He will fill you with refreshment
even when you are in a dry, difficult place.
He will continually restore strength to you,
so you will flourish like a well-watered garden

and like an ever-flowing, trustworthy spring of blessing.
Your people will rebuild long-deserted ruins,
building anew on foundations laid long before you.
You will be known as Repairers of the Cities
and Restorers of Communities."
-Isaiah 58:11-12, TPT

I received something for today's devotion that is on God's heart for you, His daughter. You have received days and days of words wooing you to the heart of Jesus. He has spoken to you tenderly and has reminded you of your value and identity and His unfathomable goodness. The reality is you can believe every single word from these last 28 days and remain on the sidelines of your calling.

As I was getting ready for the day, the Spirit whispered one word to me: "reinstate." In order to breakthrough to the open space of freedom and healing and calling, many in the Bride of Christ need to be reinstated, just like Jesus did with Peter. After this, we can be launched into all God has for us. We can't go any further in our pursuit of freedom or walking into our destiny if we don't receive and believe the Holy Spirit wants to partner together with us even with a testimony of brokenness or imperfection. In fact, He wants to not only redeem the broken things, but use them to rebuild, restore, and renew the places that have been devastated for generations. [24] There are too many women who have disqualified themselves because of brokenness, bad decisions, guilt, shame, and regret.

These parts of your story become the tools and weapons Jesus places in your hands to rebuild, plunder, take back, and conquer. These become your places of greatest authority and ministry. What if Jesus called you by name today and, just like Peter, reinstated you to take your place in history? Would you believe He could do it and set you free from the past that has held you back? Does He want to take the pain and transform it into a sword?

You bet He does! When He spoke the word "reinstate" to me, I believe with all my heart that He's ready to do it now!

If all His promises are "yes" and "amen," and if the cross is sufficient for your entire story, then you can rest assured that nothing can disqualify or sideline you. This is the resounding song of grace sung over your life. And the glorious part is that He will use you, by the power of His Spirit, to go out and find those who need to be rebuilt, restored, and renewed.

You will carry an anointing and authority to minister in a way only you can because you walked a road no one else has ever walked.

Would you receive and believe this prayer below? It's for you to be reinstated, to apply every last drop of this 31-day encounter to your story, so you can crossover to the other side.

It's time. We need you in the race. We need your voice and your authority to minister in the way only Jesus knows He can through you. Don't let the enemy take your voice or your calling any longer. Jesus will lay a new foundation of sparkling jewels, and you will be called "Repairer of the Cities, Restorer of Communities."

> Holy Spirit, I ask that You come and fill the atmosphere around each person who needs to be reinstated and commissioned. As You kneel before them, Jesus, would You put their shoes back on their feet and stand

them back up. You see the great cloud of witnesses who are cheering for their victory. You see the army hosts of heaven being released to minister and war on their behalf. You see the precious blood of Jesus applied to every memory, every wound, every word, and every pain. You speak a better word over them. You allow them to turn back and take everything the enemy meant to steal, kill, and destroy, and You will bring them all the plunder.

In the meantime, the broken foundations of their hearts and lives will be laid with precious stones that sparkle with Your glory. And they will turn with a sword in hand and go after the ones You send to them. Thank You, Holy Spirit, for this word today. Thank You for Your reinstating of my sisters! Thank You that Your Word is victory over them. Thank You that You declare healing and wholeness and freedom over them today. Thank You that their story is not done, their race is not finished, and their destiny is not determined by fear or failure or brokenness. They are readier than ever for all that is ahead because they are Yours forever, and You're faithful to complete to victory their very lives until You call them home. So, I bless them today. Together, we thank You for Your goodness, Your power, and Your presence. In Jesus' name, Amen.

Listen to this worship song via YouTube: "City of Hope" by Amanda Cook

Linda's Story

The Lord "reinstated" me on Day 28. I praise and adore Him.

At age 70 and with compromised health, I felt He wanted me to start a ladies' neighborhood prayer group in my home. I asked for at least one woman to join. I sent out 18 invitations, and one lady came the first week. We had a refreshing vibrant prayer time together.

The second week He sent more women. We are praying for the restoration of families, spiritual revival of our nation, and world evangelism and peace, among other things.

Alleluia. God is so good.

Reflections

DAY

29

REVIVAL IS COMING

"Blow the trumpet in Zion, declare a holy fast, call a sacred assembly. Gather the people, consecrate the assembly; bring together the elders, gather the children, those nursing at the breast. Let the bridegroom leave his room and the bride her chamber."

"Surely the Lord has done great things! Do not be afraid, you wild animals, for the pastures in the wilderness are becoming green. The trees are bearing their fruit; the fig tree and the vine yield their riches. Be glad, people of Zion, rejoice in the Lord your God, for he has given you the autumn rains because he is faithful. He sends you abundant showers, both autumn and spring rains, as before. The threshing floors will be filled with grain; the vats will overflow with new wine and oil."

"And afterward, I will pour out my Spirit on all people.
Your sons and daughters will prophesy,
your old men will dream dreams, your young men will see visions. Even on my servants, both men and women, I will pour out my Spirit in those days. I will show wonders in the heavens and on the earth, blood and fire and billows of smoke."

"Multitudes, multitudes in the valley of decision! For the day of the Lord is near in the valley of decision. The sun and moon will be darkened, and the stars no longer shine. The Lord will roar from Zion and thunder from Jerusalem; the earth and the heavens will tremble. But the Lord will be a refuge for his people, a stronghold for the people of Israel."
-Joel 2:15-16, 21b-24, 28-30, 3:14-16

I was reading an Instagram post from Dutch Sheets, author of "Intercessory Prayer" (excellent book, by the way). He writes, "We are going to see a tidal wave of souls coming to Jesus. We are moving into a season of evangelism such as the world has never seen. I believe we will see more saved in the next 20 years than in the last 2000 years combined. Declare that the harvest fields of the earth are ripe and the great harvest is beginning."

"'Behold, the days are coming,' declares the Lord, 'when the plowman shall overtake the reaper and the treader of grapes him who sows the seed…'"
-Amos 9:13, ESV

Do you feel the winds of revival coming? Do you feel the expectation of something significant hanging heavy in the air?

After consecrating these 31 days to the Lord and positioning ourselves in preparation for this next season, I long to hear what the Holy Spirit has spoken to you. The greatest thing we can do in this hour of preparation is worship and adore and love the One whom our lives are wrapped around. I could offer you no greater encouragement than an admonition to love Him with all that you are and all that you have. Give everything to Him as worship. Hold nothing back. Nothing else matters more than your life positioned in worship and surrender before Him.

Your life will fall into place if this foundation of worship and single-hearted pursuit is first and foremost. This is the revival of the Bride.

On a recent trip to Latin America, I shared with a family in their small little home. Before me sat four generations: a 97-year-old grandma and the next three generations. Over the course of our time together, all the family accepted Jesus except the 97-year-old grandma. They told me, "She has Alzheimer's and is out of it all the time. Just pray for her." I thought to myself, "This woman's eternity still hangs in the balance. I must share with her."

We began to pray silently that God would break through the disease and give her total clarity. As we knelt before her, the Lord did just that. She was completely aware, alert, and cognizant. And immediately she gave her life to Jesus. The Lord rescued her just in the nick of time.

He is on a rescue mission for his lost sheep, and He is sending us to go and find them and bring them back. He's sending us with His heart to those who need healing and hope and the revolutionary love of Jesus. There's a wedding feast of the Lamb that's coming, and all are invited.

Dear sisters, I implore you with all that I am to pursue Jesus with your whole heart and your whole life. Let nothing take up any place of worship in your life other than Christ alone. He will pour out His Spirit on you and raise you up in this hour to carry the mandate of heaven and the heartbeat of God. This is indeed a season of repentance and returning. This is a time where we don't carry on with life as usual. It's a new hour for the Bride of Christ.

I pray that this encounter has catalyzed a new moment and juncture in your life where things have been right set, realigned, reignited, and restored. Revival is coming. Are you ready?

> Lord, I praise You for creating the space for 31 days of consecration, preparation, and positioning. Let our lives be ignited with the fire of Your presence that the wind of the Spirit would fan into flame revival inside of us and through us. I pray that the Spirit of the Lord would rest on us. The Spirit of wisdom and of understanding. The Spirit of counsel and of power. The Spirit of knowledge and of the fear of the Lord. And I pray they will delight in the fear of the Lord (Isaiah 11:2-3).
>
> Consume every part of our lives, Jesus. Send us forth with vision and clarity and wholeness and a passion for You like we have never known before. In Jesus' name.

Listen to this worship song via YouTube: "Fall on Us" by Brandon Lake

Listen to this worship song via YouTube: "Heal our Land" by Kari Jobe

Karey's Story

Each day through this 31-day journey, I pray through the questions and I am learning how to step out in faith. Jesus is planting this in me now. He is slowly teaching me that being still is okay and sitting in His presence is all I need to do daily. Busy is not the answer.

I also know I need faith to step out into the unknown because God is the known. I may not know what He wants me to do right now, or tomorrow, or next month. But He will bring opportunities. Am I willing to step into impossible moments with Jesus, or do I sit and analyze opportunities in unbelief, fear, and intimidation?

Staying where I am and inside my comfort zone is not what God desires. He is bigger than that. He wants me and my family to be bigger than that. But He also wants us to be humble and bold in glorifying Him. He wants us to build up and strengthen others because of His blessings and the love He has shown us. He wants us to tear down walls and build up love in our heart for others, because we cannot give what we do not have.

Only He knows what we have gone through and the healing we need to be able to share His love and glory to the rest of the world. Do we trust Him? Are we ready?

Reflections

DAY 30

Running the Race

"As for us, we have all of these great witnesses who encircle us like clouds. So we must let go of every wound that has pierced us and the sin we so easily fall into. Then we will be able to run life's marathon race with passion and determination, for the path has been already marked out before us. We look away from the natural realm and we fasten our gaze onto Jesus who birthed faith within us and who leads us forward into faith's perfection. His example is this: Because his heart was focused on the joy of knowing that you would be his, he endured the agony of the cross and conquered its humiliation, and now sits exalted at the right hand of the throne of God!"
-Hebrews 12:1-2, TPT

Today's worship song expresses the hunger of my heart so perfectly. It's such a beautiful song of surrender and longing. But I want you to know in this song of hunger, the words are not determining your worth as "not enough." When God looks at you, He sees the perfection of His Son. Period. I believe the cry of the song is what we have been hearing during this journey.

Lord, I have nothing without You. You are
the absolute longing of my very life.

You have all of Jesus. He gave you all of Himself and held nothing back. We cry out for more space in us for His life to be more and more manifested through our surrender. Remember the word from Day Two. He will consume whatever we are willing to give Him. Climb up on the altar and let Him ignite you with the fire of His Holy Spirit.

Standing around us are all those who have gone before us who ran and finished their race. They passed the baton to us and are cheering for our race to be run with the victory Jesus is declaring over us. Today's theme verses have been on my heart for days, and I had to lay some things before Him before I could write this devotion.

There has been beautiful fullness through this journey, but there has also been tension in waiting to see a few things answered. In the waiting is an opportunity for unbelief or disappointment. I have contended before the Lord for months for something I believe He was having me intercede for. And to me it looks like nothing is happening.

This is the space the enemy comes in and says, "Yep, it's not. Just forget about it." Disappointment in the waiting can create a space where we lose sight of the bigger picture and our faith potentially wanes.

On my last trip to South Asia, we climbed nineteen miles up and over a mountain range. That took about nine hours straight up and three hours downhill in the dark. It was not an easy day to say the least. As we set out in the morning, we traversed thick jungle that was infested with leeches. They are so tiny and hop onto your shoes and pants as you walk through the foliage. Not only did we walk uphill, which caused rapid breathing, but I was in a sheer panic from these terrifying leeches (they get on your shoes and go through your shoes and socks to get to your skin). I couldn't get my breathing in an anaerobic rhythm; it was rapid and irregular, and I was petrified.

We ended up with leeches and survived, but these very small critters were impeding on my race that day.

We are running on the shoulders of giants who have gone before us. Many of us are finishing their assignments for this period of history. I believe that with all my heart. Jesus is living to intercede for you as you run so that you don't lose sight of your Champion of Heaven who is your very prize. So, we throw off everything that causes us to trip and we run with freedom and victory.

Metaphorically speaking, these little leeches impede my faith to believe Him when my eyes can't see the results of my contending in prayer. They keep me distracted and give an open door to the enemy to let my faith wander. As I sat with the Lord for this devotion, I journaled what I believe He wants us to hear:

> This entire 31 days has been right from My heart to My daughters. I don't want them to miss a thing. I don't want them to waste their time on what is empty and fruitless. I want them to revel in the fullness that I fill in every way because that is who I Am.
>
> I have even more for them, more than they can imagine. I have so much to show them if they will stay with Me awhile. I have called them to sit with Me in the throne room of grace and place their ear to My heart. I want to get their heart in perfect sync with Mine. I want them to feel what makes My heart skip a beat. They are My precious Bride.

> The only way they are going to be in sync with Me is to give Me the time and space in their lives to transform them and reveal to them more of who I Am. Once you have tasted the kind of love I give, you will never long for the love of another. I fill everything to overflowing in every way. That is who I Am and I will do it.

As we end our time of consecration together, I join my voice with those who encircle you to run to the One lover of your soul. Find your satisfaction, hope, and delight in Him. He will never disappoint. He is answering when we pray, and He is trustworthy and moving with great acceleration.

So, don't lose sight. Don't lose hope. He's on the move and at the finish line. Fix your eyes and position your heart. These are days of rigorous preparation for "that day" when all of history culminates at the Wedding Feast of the Lamb.

Listen to this worship song via YouTube: "Here Again" by Rheva Henry

Maya's Story

The day of this devotional, I woke up from a strange dream. I was trying to watch the finish of a bike race, but two times I had been at the wrong spot and didn't see the finish. I went to look for the race and found a running race instead. That's when it clicked for me. I keep looking for the wrong finish, the wrong race. God is working – just not the way I expect Him to work.

I have been praying for my husband's spine issues, and God has answered those prayers. But not in the way I thought. Our daughter has problems with gluten, so my husband joined her on a gluten-free diet. His digestive issues and psoriasis went away. Though it's just a step toward complete healing, I'm encouraged. I feel like God keeps telling me His ways are higher than mine, and His answers don't always come the way I imagine.

When this 31-day journey began, our family was traveling back from Slovakia. I was discouraged by the comfortable seats offered in business class knowing that our family would be in economy seating, squished into tiny seats with no way to stretch out. My thoughts were, "If God wants to, He can give us nice business class seats." Instead, God gave each of us an entire row of seats so we could lay down in the economy section. Again, His answer was different than I imagined, yet so much better.

God is on the move and at the finish line. I just need to fix my eyes and position my heart on Him.

Reflections

DAY

31

Ready, Set, Go!

"Then Jesus came close to them and said, 'All the authority of the universe has been given to me. Now go in my authority and make disciples of all nations, baptizing them in the name of the Father, the Son, and the Holy Spirit. And teach them to faithfully follow all that I have commanded you. And never forget that I am with you every day, even to the completion of this age."

-Matthew 28:18-20, TPT

"And he said to them, 'As you go into all the world, preach openly the wonderful news of the gospel to the entire human race! Whoever believes the good news and is baptized will be saved, and whoever does not believe the good news will be condemned. And these miracle signs will accompany those who believe: They will drive out demons in the power of my name. They will speak in tongues. They will be supernaturally protected from snakes and from drinking anything poisonous. And they will lay hands on the sick and heal them.' After saying these things, Jesus was lifted up into heaven and sat down at the place of honor at the right hand of God! And the apostles went out announcing the good news everywhere, as the Lord himself consistently worked with them, validating the message they preached with miracle-signs that accompanied them!"

-Mark 16:15-20, TPT

Today's song fits perfectly for the close of our month of consecration and preparation. This season has been a miracle on many levels, and there is more to come.

I knew I would close with two commissioning passages in Scripture. It's as though our time culminates in these two passages - the words Jesus left us before He sat at the right hand of the Father. In them, He decreed our authority is the authority of Christ which He gave without limitation. He gave us the promise of His presence and the manifestation of His goodness in and through our lives without any limitation. He promised us that there would be confirmation to what was preached with signs and wonders demonstrating God's love to a desperate world. These disciples were the most unlikely group to birth a global movement of impossibility, but it didn't matter because they were sealed and sent with the promise and the power of the Holy Spirit.

> "Understanding that you are a son or daughter of God and knowing how lavishly the Father loves you is what makes you free to enter your destiny. Only this can give you confidence enough to say *'YES'* to the fullness of the call God will put in your heart. If you can catch even a glimpse of how warmly God smiles upon you, you will want to give Him everything for the rest of your life. You will go to the ends of the earth for Him. Whether it means living in the dirt with the poorest of poor or being salt and light to Harvard elites, we are all called to shine in our own way. God has a special pair of shoes just for you, perfectly suited for your own path. You must learn to wear your own shoes and never put on anyone else's. Walk in your anointing." -Heidi Baker [25]

Your commissioning will begin when you believe that He actually created you with a destiny that was written before the foundations of the world were formed. He knew the skills, brilliance, creativity, giftedness, personality, location, realm of influence, weaknesses, and frailties you bear. Just like these fishermen, whom Jesus invited to begin their impossible, He is inviting you into a new chapter of even greater things. We move from glory to glory, and there's no time like now to invite Him to captain your ship and do every impossible thing in your life.

Disciples are made through teaching and learning. As we walked through the Word and entered into places of worship together, I implore you to be a self-feeder. To those who fasted sleep to be with Jesus, don't let up! Continue to stretch out to find even more time to be with Him, the Lover of your soul. Find other hungry people and surround yourself with them. Who you surround yourself with is key to your discipleship.

It was uncommon for the Jews at that time to go out to see nations. Their commissioning was revolutionary. They had to begin to see people outside of the Jewish culture. They stayed continually at the temple worshiping after Jesus ascended. It took a couple of years for this group to "go!" The scene was catalyzed by persecution and the little birds were flung from their nest. They had to fly. I love our Bible studies and times of corporate worship and equipping, but that's not the full picture. All of that is in preparation for the daily "go" we are called to.

> "Now is the time for sons and daughters of God to be revealed, who will not only preach the glorious gospel but will radically live it. These people are a new breed rising up in the earth today. They are simple people who will change the world one day and one person at

a time. They are people possessed by love. They are free from fear. They are bold. They are kind. They are patient. They are powerful. They are humble, and they are joyful. They associate with the poor and dine with Kings. Wherever they go, they start revivals … or riots. They are often mistaken for angels or gods. They are a holy people. They are righteous. They are unusual. They move and blow like the wind. They are feared, they are loved, and they are hated all at the same time. They are often misunderstood. They are neither puffed up by the praises of man nor torn down by criticism. How can they be? They know they are loved. They are ordinary people who have been possessed by an extraordinary God. They look like God. They act like God. They love like God. They are born of God. They are filled with God." -Peter Louis[26]

Beloved, that's you. You bear the name of Jesus. You embody Christ Himself through the Holy Spirt. He indwells you. You have been called and commissioned to arise and go storm the gates of hell. We don't take anything to Heaven with us except people, so go and find them. Let your life be the living demonstration and proclamation of the gospel.

As we end this time together, I want to commission some of you specifically.

To my sisters who are 60 and older, we need you in the race. You are critical to the Bride of Christ. We need your wisdom and your discipleship. We need you to bring up women who are younger than you and pour into their lives. I commission you to equip and send forth younger generations.

To my sisters who are nurses, doctors, and counselors, I commission you to manifest the Healer who lives inside of you.

To my sisters who are apostles, prophets, evangelists, pastors, and teachers, I commission you to advance. Do not retreat. This is the moment the Holy Spirit has called you to. Build up the Bride of Christ on a global level.

To my sisters who are intercessors for the nations, realms of society, and the Church in this hour, rally more women to your prayer closet with you. I commission you to train up others in intercession. We need watchmen on the wall like never before.

To our Lydias, I commission you to work with all your might, in the power of Jesus, to build the Kingdom of God here on earth.

To my sisters who are moms, I commission you to raise world changers and history makers. Raise them to know the Lord in deep intimacy and worship. Show them what this looks like from your very life.

To my sisters who are creators, inventors, writers, designers, and artists, you are made in the image of a very creative and brilliant God. I commission you to reveal the depth and marvel of who God is in all you create and bring forth from your hands, minds, and mouths!

To my sisters who lead worship and bring others before the throne of Grace, I commission you to deeper intimacy with the Lord. I ask the Lord to anoint your mind, spirit, and heart to hear the songs that are being sung in heaven and to release them here on earth.

To my precious sisters who feel really broken right now, I commission you to step into your healing, wholeness, and breakthrough. Let God redeem every part of your story. He's roaring for you. You will be the fiercest and bravest ones in this race.

To all my sisters who are commissioned to "go" (that is every one of you reading this), I commission you to dive in over your head into the perfect love of God for you. May you never crawl back up on shore but swim in the sea of His grace and goodness and invite others to plunge on in with you until He takes us home.

Thank you for the honor and privilege of worship and wonder together. You have my heart and my intercession. Arise, dear daughters of the Most High God. Your time is now.

Listen to this worship song via YouTube: "Miracle" by Mosiac MSC, led by LWW

Leila's Story

"Jesus, You know my desire for grandchildren despite not being blessed with children of our own. You also know my heart for people from other nations. As we relocate from Dallas to a much smaller college town, would You bless me with grandchildren? Would You give us friendships with people from other cultures and nations? Would You bless our home to be a safe place for connection for all who come and for those who need family there?"

God's answer to my prayer was hilarious! Rather than sending us to the nations, He sent the nations to us. An Indian couple, both Ph.D.s in the vet school, became our neighbors. The husband follows his childhood religion and the wife considers herself an atheist but "would be praying louder than anyone if the plane was going down." They have both lost their mothers. The have two sons, ages 6 and 8 months. She asked us to be the surrogate grandparents. We have had conversations about faith, and they know and respect where we stand.

Additionally, a young Turkish couple joined the engineering faculty and moved into our neighborhood. We met and enjoyed time with them while they were moving in. I met the grandmothers of their 3-year-old daughter, but I get to be the stand-in grandmother while they are here.

God is so good. He answered my prayer for grandchildren with two Indian grandsons and a Turkish granddaughter. My multicultural heart adores that! There are many international faculty members in our neighborhood. My husband's Ph.D. is a connecting point along with my gift of hospitality in bringing desserts to people as they move in. We are blessed to get to be a part of ministering to the nations while staying in our own neighborhood.

Reflections

Conclusion

The only way I know to conclude these 31 days together, in the secret place with Jesus, is to pray for you, if you will permit me to do so.

> Lord, I bless Your name. Your name that is above all other names. And to even believe that we bear Your name. We are marked by it, commissioned by it, renamed by it, and healed forever by Your precious blood and Your glorious name.
>
> I pray for those reading the pages You spoke to me as I sat with You hours and hours each day. Lord, would You ignite in these fiery ones a spirit of revival that would demonstrate the invitation and captivation of love You have for Your people who bear Your image.
>
> I pray that the church would arise in this hour, full of the life of Christ You died to give to us, that now resides inside of those who have been made Yours. I pray for a mantle of courage and boldness to proclaim and demonstrate Your goodness. Give them a conviction that You are enough for them. I pray that You would miraculously change their appetites and cravings to long for only You, Jesus. I pray that lives would be radically shifted to pursue Your heart and Your

purposes right now, in this time in history. Unleash our history makers, young and old, with clarity, discernment, wisdom, vision, and immovability. May they abound in the things You have destined for them before the foundations of the world were set in motion.

I bless those reading this and ask for acceleration, increase, and wonder to be the road marked before them, in Jesus' name. May their lives be a house of prayer for all nations, both interceding, inviting, and traversing roads to find the people waiting to hear the glorious good news.

Lord, may our churches look different- blow the four walls down. May unity be our benchmark in our cities. May our lives be wholly aligned with Your purposes only; not man-made strategy for church growth. I pray for a call to holiness, a fear of the Lord, and an agreement with Your purposes, and Your purposes alone. May everything else fall into submission to what You are speaking over Your people and Your church right now. This is the place where we soar in Your fullness and goodness and our true identity. Tuck us into that reality, I pray, in Jesus' precious and matchless name.

Don't waste one day living outside of a passionate, courageous, and bold life of following Jesus. He's worth it all!

If any of these days have spoken to you, I would love to hear from you. You can email me at jking@eastwest.org.

Your fellow fiery one,
Julie King

About the Author

Julie King has been married to Michael for 25 years. They have had the privilege of watching their four daughters - Elizabeth, Emily, AnnMarie, and Grace - grow and develop a passion for Jesus and have a heart for the nations. Her family is the delight of her life.

Julie grew up a missionary kid to parents who served on staff with CRU for 33 years. Much of her youth was spent living overseas in Germany, during the fall of the Berlin Wall and the opening of the Iron Curtain. It was a formative period for both her worldview and passion for the gospel. Today Julie leads women around the world to take the gospel to people who have never heard the name of Jesus.

As an adult, Julie's desire and passion for the Bride of Christ and the lost, those who don't know Jesus personally, compelled her to begin a neighborhood Bible study to engage others in the Word and on mission. One result of this initiative was a prayer and worship gathering in Frisco, Texas called *God of the City: The Church unified-revived-unleashed.* This three-year planting of the Lord was a movement to unite the church in North Dallas for the purpose of worship and prayer for revival. Hundreds of churches participated in the event, which was attended by thousands.

In 2018, Julie began an initiative called Arise through the mission of East-West Ministries International. Through this effort, she is seeing women grow in a depth of hunger and passion for Jesus and His heart for the world.

Julie has a passion for the Word and for worship and loves rallying people to the very things God brings forth in her spirit. This book is a result of those passions, and she believes there's more to come!

About East-West Ministries International

East-West began because two men couldn't resist the call of Christ's great mission: go into the world and make disciples (Matthew 28:18-20).

Through their work behind the Iron Curtain in the early 1980s, East-West founders, John Maisel and Bud Toole, recognized the profound need to train church planters and pastors in nations with severely restricted Christian activity.

In May 1993, East-West Ministries International was established to train and mentor faithful and reliable national pastors to become catalysts for indigenous church growth - reaching the lost with the gospel, equipping new believers, and multiplying reproducible churches.

Today, East-West works primarily in limited access countries and among unreached people groups throughout 54 countries worldwide so that disciples and churches will continuously multiply.

VISION: The vision of East-West is to glorify God by multiplying followers of Jesus in the spiritually darkest areas of the world.

MISSION: We exist to mobilize the Body of Christ to evangelize the lost and equip local believers to multiply disciples and healthy churches among unreached peoples and/or in restricted access communities.

GET INVOLVED: To learn more about East-West or to join our global ministry, visit www.eastwest.org/get-involved.

About Arise

Arise is an initiative born out of East-West's desire to empower women around the world to be used by God to take the gospel to the nations. This is done by calling, connecting, and commissioning them to one another and to the heart and purposes of God in this hour.

There is a call from the Lord for women right now to live in the authority and identity given to them by Christ. We are connecting women to each other through stories and experiences. And women are being commissioned to be a powerful force for the Kingdom of God.

That's why Arise exists.

We have hopeful expectation that as we call women to live boldly in the power of the Holy Spirit, connect them to each other for ongoing encouragement, and send them out on their unique mission, a culture of revival will break loose as families, communities, and nations are changed forever for the glory of God.

Why? Because it's happened in the past.

Through women of our ancient past (like Deborah, Ruth, Mary, and Lydia) and women of recent centuries (like Joan of Arc, Amy Carmichael, Corrie ten Boom, Mother Teresa, and Heidi Baker) God changed the world.

We believe that women who are moved by a passionate love for Jesus and who partner with Him to build His Kingdom are a key to unlocking gospel movements in the world's spiritually dark places.

To learn more or to get involved with Arise, visit www.eastwest.org/arise.

NOTES

How to Use This Book

i Laura Vawser. *The Prophetic Voice of God: Learning to Recognize the Language of the Holy Spirit.* (Shippensburg, PA: Destiny Image Publishers, Inc., 2018)

Day One | Are You Ready? Here We Go!

1 Daniel 2:22

2 Ephesians 5:2 (NIRV)

Day Three | Drawing into His Heart

3 Luke 1:37 (TPT)

Day Four | This Moment Right Now

4 Jeremiah 20:9

Day Six | Bringing the Promise

5 1 Kings 18:41

6 1 Kings 18:42

Day Seven | Worship 'til There's Breakthrough

7 2 Samuel 6:14-22

Day Eight | Come Back to Me

8 Romans 8:1

Day Twelve | Revival and Romance

9 Psalm 126

Day Thirteen | He is Coming!

10 Matthew 25:1-13

Day Sixteen | It's Time to Ascend

11 Romans 12:1-2

Day Seventeen | You Will Cross Over

12 Mark 4:11

13 Mark 4:25

14 Mark 4:35 (TPT)

Day Eighteen | Daughter of Mine

15 Psalm 34

Day Nineteen | His Voice and Your Voice

16 James 3

17 Laura Vawser. *The Prophetic Voice of God: Learning to Recognize the Language of the Holy Spirit.* (Shippensburg, PA: Destiny Image Publishers, Inc., 2018)

Day Twenty | I Will See a Victory

18 1 Chronicles 18:14-17

Day Twenty-Two | His Resurrection … Your Commissioning

19 Mindi Oaten Art, www.MindiOaten.com

Day Twenty-Three | Awaken and Arise

20 John 14:12

Day Twenty-Five | Arise, our Lydias

21 https://www.biblegateway.com/devotionals/all-women-bible/3830/08/02. Assessed 2/19/2020

22 Vallotton, Kris. *Fashioned to Reign,* (Bloomington, MN: Chosen Books, 2013) p. 101.

Day Twenty-Six | Let Your Faith Testify

23 Paul's ministry was from 36AD-68AD

Day Twenty-Eight | It's Time to be "Reinstated"

[24] Isaiah 61:4

Day Thirty-One | Ready, Set, Go!

[25] Baker, Heidi. *Birthing the Miraculous,* (Lake Mary, FL: Charisma House, 2014) p. 85

[26] Louis, Peter. *Back to the Gospel: Reviving the Church through the Message that Birthed It.* (2016) p. 178

WORKS CITED

Baker, Heidi. *Birthing the Miraculous,* (Lake Mary, FL: Charisma House, 2014) p. 85

Louis, Peter. *Back to the Gospel: Reviving the Church through the Message that Birthed It.* (2016) p. 178

Vallotton, Kris. *Fashioned to Reign,* (Bloomington, MN: Chosen Books, 2013) p. 101.

Vawser, Laura. *The Prophetic Voice of God: Learning to Recognize the Language of the Holy Spirit.* (Shippensburg, PA: Destiny Image Publishers, Inc., 2018)

Made in the USA
Middletown, DE
21 June 2021

42755157R00137